GILES PLAYFAIR

CRIME

IN OUR CENTURY

MANSON, Charles M.
AKA: "Jesus Christ"
"God"
WATSON, Charles Denton
AKA: MONTGOMERY, Tex
"Texas Charlie"
PHOTO 5780
VAN HOUTEN, Leslie
AKA: SANKSTON, Leslie
PHOTO 5755
KRENWINKLE, Patricia
AKA: SCOTT, Mary Ann
REEVES, Marnie Kay

By the same author:

My Father's Son
Kean
Singapore Goes Off the Air
The Heart of Fame
The Little Tour
(with Constantine FitzGibbon)
The Offenders
(with Derrick Sington)
Crime, Punishment and Cure
(with Derrick Sington)
The Prodigy
Six Studies in Hypocrisy
The Punitive Obsession

First published in Great Britain in 1977 by
Sidgwick and Jackson Limited

ISBN 0 283 98310 8

Designed by Paul Watkins
Picture research by the Popperfoto Library

Printed in Great Britain by
The Garden City Press Limited
Letchworth, Hertfordshire SG6 1JS

for Sidgwick and Jackson Limited
1 Tavistock Chambers, Bloomsbury Way
London WC1A 2SG

CONTENTS

INTRODUCTION

The average man may be a 'criminal' in the sense that he has, knowingly or unknowingly, broken the law at some moment in his life. But it is also true that the more serious the crime, the less he is *tempted* to commit it, and not so much from fear of the consequences as from the guidance of his conscience. If this were not so, no organized society could exist.

It follows that punishment operates on a steadily declining scale of effectiveness until it reaches the point, short of killing the culprit or locking him up for the rest of his natural life, of total uselessness. Governments do not admit this, of course. Nevertheless, it is the underlying point of all the more or less notorious cases with which I have chosen to deal.

But what, to begin with, is crime?

It might be defined as any form of behaviour that the law disallows; of course, what is against the law depends to a certain extent upon where one happens to live. The difference in this respect between a democratic and an authoritarian society needs no stressing, but even within the so-called free world there are considerable divergencies. Thus in both Britain and the United States incest used to be regarded until recently as an unusually repulsive crime. But in France, and other countries governed by the Napoleonic code, incest has long been indulged in by adults with complete impunity. Again, in Britain, adultery, though it was until very modern times considered a grave sin, has never been a crime. In France, on the other hand, as in the large majority of American jurisdictions, it remains, under certain circumstances, punishable by the state.

Since I have not wished to argue the question of whether particular acts should or should not be illegal, I have confined my attention to those forms of behaviour, such as espionage and murder, which are held to be seriously criminal no matter where they take place. The crimes I have described belong to the present century, and are largely drawn from England and America. With one exception—it concerns a man who was murdered before justice caught up with him—they all ended in more or less heavy punishment. But I do not refer to the punishment in order to laud it. On the contrary, I am persuaded that in each and every instance the punishment was misguided.

This is not to claim that all the defendants were wrongfully convicted; as a matter of fact, apart from two probables and three faintly possibles, they were all, pretty certainly, guilty. But, to state it bluntly, while I am opposed to the death penalty under any and all circumstances, I am only to a degree less opposed to *punitive* imprisonment. And in saying this, I am not considering the criminal at the expense of the victim. I place the prevention of serious crime, and hence the protection of the community against it, above every other consideration. But this is not something which in my view can be accomplished by locking people up for greater or lesser periods wholly or even partially as a punishment.

There are murderers (or supposed murderers) in two other parts of the book—those dealing with organized crime and political crime—besides the part devoted to murder as such. In the last-named part I have included a chapter that deals with murderers whom I describe as being grossly abnormal. Of these, two escaped execution in England and three in California only because of the ending of capital punishment.

As a matter of fact, the question of the mental competence of an accused person, whatever the nature of his offence, seldom arises at all unless he himself chooses to put it at issue, and the judge who will pass sentence on him cannot look beyond the stated motive of his crime, which is purposely made as simply understood as possible so as not to confuse the jury. A recent English case provides an illustration of this.

Alastair Steadman was convicted in September 1975 of attempting to sell secrets to the Russians. The judge seemed in no doubt that his act should be regarded as a perfectly normal, if exceptionally disgraceful, type of crime. In passing sentence of nine years' imprisonment on Steadman, he told him: 'You have been found guilty on quite overwhelming evidence of a deliberate attempt to betray your country. Over a period of years you have been trained as a highly skilled officer in the Air Force. You were prepared to turn traitor if the money was right, as you put it. I do not propose to waste further time on you.'[1]

Yet, to judge from the television and newspaper coverage after Steadman had been sentenced, the public was prepared to 'waste' a considerable amount of 'further time' on him. According to one account, Steadman was a sort of Captain Queeg, the fictional psychopath of *The Caine Mutiny*. He was so obsessed with his dreams of becoming a multi-millionaire property developer that when he was in command in the air he appeared hardly aware of what his mission was supposed to be. For nearly a year his long-suffering crew covered for him, but at last decided they would have to report his extraordinarily negligent behaviour. As a result, he was grounded pending an inquiry. When the inquiry took place, he blamed everyone else but himself, and after appealing unsuccessfully to the Air Council was eventually forced to resign or face being cashiered. It was then that he resolved on his plan of selling secrets: a plan (so he childishly imagined) which would at once gather the millions he dreamed of getting and wreak vengeance on the R.A.F. for its (in his view) gross ill-treatment of him.

Other similar stories were told by the media; and all of them suggested a far more complicated motive than had been apparent from the court proceedings. Though none of these stories questioned the propriety of the sentence, they did seem to show that this crime was more pathological than normal. Even so, it is certain that Steadman could never have raised a successful insanity plea in an English court, though in the United States (he would be subject to federal law), where wider latitude is allowed, he might possibly have succeeded with a clever enough lawyer, who could have allied him dramatically with Captain Queeg. Whether he himself would have chosen to risk being found mentally incompetent is, of course, another matter.

In England there is a defence known as 'diminished responsibility', which was borrowed from Scottish law. For some unexplained and quite possibly inexplicable reason, it can be used only against a charge of murder. But this defence, if it succeeds, merely serves to obtain a conviction of manslaughter rather than murder, and does not necessarily, or by any means invariably, excuse the defendant from liability to punishment. So far as the law is concerned, it would seem that a deviance or abnormal impulse or drive can be properly or at any rate logically called uncontrollable only if the accused person successfully pleads insanity (if he is very mad he may be adjudged unfit to plead) and is, therefore, held to be not guilty on that account.

But, here again, there is no agreement about what legal insanity means. The definitions vary all the way from a virtual non-definition in the state of New Hampshire, where it is held that a man should be considered unpunishable if his act was the 'offspring or product of mental disease', to the strict M'Naghten Rule, originating in English law, which lays it down that a man is insane if 'at the time of the committing of the act [he] was labouring under such a defect of reason, from disease of the mind, as not to know the nature and quality of the act he was doing or, if he did know it, that he did not know it was wrong'. In the case of Durham v. United States, the Court of Appeals for the District of Columbia formulated a non-definition like that of New Hampshire: 'an accused person is not criminally responsible if his unlawful act was the product of mental disease or defect.' Otherwise, the American jurisdictions are nominally governed by the M'Naghten test, except that some fifteen of them also permit 'irresistible impulse' as a defence.

I have not included in this book any instances of uncontrollable behaviour which the law in either country recognized as such through finding the accused person insane. I was, however, very tempted to examine the case of Harry K. Thaw, the upstart millionaire (he was called an upstart at the time) who murdered the brilliant architect Stanford White in New York near the beginning of the century. Though Thaw eventually won his release from a mental hospital and died peacefully and at liberty in 1947, I don't doubt that he was deranged; his wild autobiography called *The Traitor,* which he had published at his own expense in New York in 1926, is quite enough to indicate it. But I question whether he would ever have passed the M'Naghten test in England or, for that matter, escaped the electric chair in New York, if he had been a poor man instead of a very rich one.

He was certainly not as mad as Ronald True, who some years later was found guilty and sentenced to death in an English court, though he was subsequently reprieved and transferred to Broadmoor mental hospital, where he remained for the rest of his life. Certainly, Thaw was sanity itself at the time of the crime, compared with the wretched child murderer Albert Fish, who pleaded not guilty in New York by reason of insanity long after Thaw had been set free and was nonetheless executed. Still the fact remains that Thaw was sent to a mental hospital, and thus his case is irrelevant to my theme.

As I have said, some of the murderers I deal with in this book, though adjudged legally sane, were grossly abnormal, which is to say that they were undeterrable by any threat of punishment, however severe. If anybody doubts this, let him consider the following proposition. Suppose a law were to be passed which furnished the judiciary with a discretionary power to give every murderer, no matter how repulsive his crime, a second chance on the understanding that if he were to murder again he would indubitably be executed. What judge would use this discretion in favour of a Haigh or a Manson?

It is surely plain that people of this fortunately very rare sort have never been deterred by any form of punishment, nor could they be now. A secure mental hospital is where they should be confined until such time (if it ever comes) when medical science has discovered the means of making them safe. Although its conditions could certainly be improved, the secure hospital does *not* exist as a punishment in theory or wholly in practice. When a man is isolated from society for the rest of his life—and this seems to be the likely fate of those grossly abnormal murderers who have been sentenced to life imprisonment—he should be permitted as much freedom as can reasonably be allowed him within the limitation of his safekeeping. It would be kinder to kill him than to subject him, continuously, to the deadening hand of ordinary prison conditions.

In fact, this seems to me the one sound argument in favour of restoring (or keeping) the death penalty! The prolonged discussion, which rumbles on and on, about its deterrent effectiveness is, I feel sure, an irrelevance. For the truth is that even if it could be proved that the death penalty was uniquely effective as a deterrent, that would be an insufficient justification for its use. If this were not so, the problem of death or injury on the roads—a more formidable problem in itself than murder—might be solved by threatening mandatory capital punishment for dangerous driving. But historically the general tendency has been to make punishment milder and milder. It would be inconceivable today to restore drawing and quartering (abolished well under 200 years ago), however deterrent that might be or was represented to be, or, for that matter, to toughen up life imprisonment (as the alternative to death penalty) by the reintroduction of such things as perpetual solitary confinement, the crank and the treadwheel. And why? Because they strike us, all of us (the lunatic fringe excepted), as barbarities. So, inevitably, sooner probably than later, will the death penalty.

Yet we still cling to the idea that the only possible response to serious crime without capital punishment is imprisonment. And imprisonment is, as it has been for at least the past century and a half, supposed to serve both the purposes of retribution-deterrence (punishment) and reform. These purposes are mutually incompatible. Bernard Shaw put the point as clearly as it can be put in his preface to the Webbs' book, *English Prisons under Local Government*.[2]

. . . To punish and reform people by the same operation is exactly as if you were to take a man suffering from pneumonia, and attempt to combine punitive and curative treatment. Arguing that a man with pneumonia is a danger to the community, and that he need not catch the disease if he takes proper care of his health, you resolve that he shall have a severe lesson, both to punish him for his negligence and pulmonary weakness, and to deter others from following his example. You therefore strip him naked, and in that condition stand him all night in the snow. But as you admit the duty of restoring him to health if possible, and discharging him with sound lungs, you engage a doctor to superintend the punishment and administer cough lozenges made as unpleasant as possible so as not to pamper the culprit. A Board of Commissioners ordering such a treatment would prove thereby that either they were imbeciles or else they were hotly in earnest about punishing the patient and not in the least in earnest about curing him . . . When our Prison Commissioners pretend to combine punishment with moral reformation they are in the same dilemma. We are told that the reformation of the criminal is kept constantly in view; yet the destruction of the prisoner's self-respect by systematic humiliation is deliberately ordered and practised . . . .

Although those words were written more than fifty years ago, nothing has changed since, except that England no longer has a Prison Commission. If catching pneumonia were to be made a criminal offence where negligence could be proved, a judge would understandably feel betrayed if a guilty invalid whom he has sent to prison were treated in precisely the same way as an innocent one who had gone to hospital of his own accord or had been sent there by the local health authorities. In other words *punishment* by imprisonment, if it is to have the meaning which the law ascribes to it, must involve the infliction of suffering.

Of course, it can be argued that however unfair (and uncivilized) it may be to keep any criminal in punitive custody for as long as he may live, it does serve the purpose of crime prevention. And it so happens that some, though not all, of the murderers I have chosen as illustrations either would have belonged, if they hadn't been executed, or belong today in this category. So do certain other types of criminal whose cases I could well have chosen, such as the rapist who is too disturbed to help himself or even, in the present state of medical knowledge, to be treatable. He may be sent to prison for life with the judge's recommendation (in England) that in his case life must mean life.

But if he is kept in prison for good at least society has the satisfaction of knowing that it is safe from him. By contrast, the great majority of prison sentences are, and many of them can only be, for fixed terms, or in America for terms fixed between maximum and minimum limits; and their length depends in general not on what sort of man the culprit is, or what kind of curative treatment he may need, but in part on his past criminal record and in part on the nature of the offence he has now been found guilty of. This (if I may continue with the Shavian analogy) is if anything rather more foolish than sentencing a man suffering from pneumonia to a fixed term in bed.

Under the English Mental Health Act of 1959 a judge is empowered to make a hospital order in the case of an offender suffering from 'mental illness, psychopathic disorder, subnormality or severe subnormality'. A clergyman was recently given a seven-year sentence in prison for robbery, despite his plea of guilty and psychiatric evidence that he was suffering from psychopathic disorder and should be sent to a mental hospital for an indefinite time. The judge decided (on what grounds one cannot imagine) to ignore the psychiatric advice and to allow the clergyman a determinate period of punishment to learn his lesson. 'You are perfectly capable of behaving in a proper Christian manner if you want to,' he told this man whom he had never met and of whom he could have known nothing before the trial.

In another somewhat worse case a man pleaded guilty to indecent behaviour towards small boys, and said that he had frequently begged in vain for psychiatric help. The judge, in returning him to prison for another long stretch, remarked that the only cure for what ailed him was 'self-control'. Even if that were true, prison could hardly be expected either to teach or encourage him to exercise it after his next release.

There are so-called psychiatric prisons, like Grendon Underwood in England and Vacaville in California, but to attach the word 'psychiatric' to the word 'prison' is hardly less absurd than the pretence that you can reform and punish by the same operation. For the majority of the 'patients' are bound at some pre-determined moment to be released, whether they have improved or not. In 1969, a psychiatric wing was set up at the tough maximum security English prison of Parkhurst, and there especially dangerous psychopaths are held, nearly all of them believed to be incurable. Yet more than half are serving fixed sentences and will have to be returned to the community, where they will be free to plunder and kill, as soon as their release becomes due. The same thing is true in America, where some prisons have one or more psychiatrists working in them.

But in themselves the judges are not primarily to blame for this scandal—and it is no less. The real fault lies with society, which, though it is thereby endangering itself, still prefers to punish offenders who are plainly too disturbed to have control of their actions rather than provide the necessary resources, human and financial, to treat those of them who may be curable and to make sure that the others are given a reasonably decent existence. It is the 'worst' cases—those that, understandably perhaps, arouse the greatest desire for vengeance among large sections of society—that in my view are the most deserving of humane treatment rather than death by execution or imprisonment. I have been guided by this consideration in my choice of cases, which includes that of the Kray twins and the press-named 'Mad Axeman' in the part dealing with organized crime, as well as Manson and the rest in the chapter on horrific murders.

Now I am not suggesting, as a few liberally minded people do suggest, that all serious criminals are mentally disturbed. I have no reason to believe that Crippen, for instance, was. I do insist, however, on two things. First, a sensible society, a society honestly concerned about means of preventing crime, should devote itself uncompromisingly to curing rather than punishing lawbreakers whom it feels bound to deprive of their liberty. Secondly, abnormality need not necessarily be equated with mental abnormality. It can be—it frequently is—what may be broadly described as social abnormality, that is a radical departure from behaviour which society as a whole considers tolerable.

Thus the crime of murder has rightly been called an intolerably 'abnormal' act, no matter how 'normal' the person who commits it may appear to be, so that anyone found guilty of murder would have to be deprived of his liberty automatically—that is to say be placed in a restricted environment, but one free of needlessly oppressive rules and regulations in the interests of deterrence, until he had given satisfactory evidence that he could safely be set free. It seems unlikely that Crippen would ever have offended again, but there certainly could have been no prospect of releasing him until he had faced, and learned to live with, the truth about himself.

Similarly with William Podmore, a petty thief turned murderer, who, like Crippen, died protesting his innocence. Their cases could possibly, though not necessarily, have been handled by a psychiatrist; but clearly Sacco and Vanzetti would have needed someone to attend to them with an entirely different approach. Either, they would have convinced this someone that they had nothing to do with the murder of Berardelli, or they would eventually have confessed to it and repented. In the latter case, they were (as I suggest) terrorists, and the only way of curing them would have been by talking them out of their convictions, just as it would have been the only way of curing the Rosenbergs (assuming their guilt) or Jim Richards, the Irish terrorist convicted of murder. This would doubtless be objected to as 'brain-washing'. But brain-washing of this sort would surely have been far less objectionable than killing them or, as would be done today presumably, locking them up for their literal lives under the punitive conditions of imprisonment.

Anyone convicted of murder should, in my view, be automatically deprived of liberty. Anyone convicted of a crime of violence, or a crime against the state, should be *prima facie* liable, and so should repeaters of serious crime. Their sentence should be for an indefinite period—it should last for as long or as short a time as is considered necessary—and should be suited to their particular needs. They should be regarded as unpunishable, and deprivation of liberty should be something entirely distinct from imprisonment—something without unnecessary 'pains'. At the same time, it should be said that this is something most people would fear as they fear entering a hospital for an indefinite stay, and fear a good deal more than a fixed prison sentence. Loss of freedom is, after all, the supreme deterrent, however it may be imposed.

But there are serious cases with which I deal (and again I could have chosen others) which might have been adequately dealt with, at any rate in the first place, by the use of the punitive powers that I would allow the courts to retain. Punishment would consist of a fine or enforced social service or both. Although I believe that even punishment of this kind is objectionable inasmuch as it may be hurtful to the innocent as well as the guilty, I am unable to accept the idea that society could afford to do without open deterrents. At least this form of punishment would not be socially self-defeating.

A fining system to be properly effective would have

to be given teeth, and this would entail the substitution of 'punishment to fit the crime' by 'punishment to fit both the crime and the criminal'. Sweden, Portugal and several Latin American states already use 'day-fines': fines, that is, which are prescribed by law on the basis of the offender's daily wage or other source of daily income. If this idea were to be extended, *all* fines would take the form, not of a set monetary sum, but of a maximum and minimum percentage of an offender's income for a month, a year or longer (over and above what he could show was necessary for his bare subsistence) and a levy on his capital, if he had any. Since steps would be taken to prevent an offender from making over money to his wife, or vice versa, this would insure that the rich could no more afford to break the law by, say, fraudulent conversion than could the poor by petty theft.

A suitably large fine is the punishment that should have been imposed, in my opinion, on the English swindlers Clarence Hatry, Leopold Harris and Horatio Bottomley, provided they had been additionally sentenced to some form of social service. In Hatry's case, and very likely in Harris's as well, it would have succeeded in its purpose and avoided the total waste of a large portion of their lives. The punishment might have been even harder for Bottomley to bear, especially if he had any genuine belief in his own fantasy of innocence, than the five years he spent in prison. But from society's point of view, it would have been constructive, and, incidentally, profitable instead of costly.

A similar sentence would have had to be tried on the confidence trickster Victor Lustig (since, remarkably, he had no previous convictions in the U.S.A.), though I am extremely doubtful that it could have succeeded. He would probably have vanished to pursue his activities under another alias, and it would then have been a question of waiting until he was caught again before moving to deprive him of his liberty. He was, as I show, a fantasist, and he might well have responded to some form of psychiatric treatment. Anyhow, it was fortunate for American society that he died in prison before completing his twenty-year term, for if he had lived to come out again he would almost certainly have reverted to his career of fraud.

The Mayfair Boys, who carried out the jewel theft at the Hyde Park Hotel in 1937, would have been *prima facie* liable to deprivation of liberty, because their crime involved violence. But, though it is clearly impossible to be certain of this, punishment would quite likely have been effective in their case, especially if they had been ordered a long and sufficiently hard period of community service. What they did was, of course, shocking. But however shocking the thing a person does, and however responsible he may be for his actions, imprisonment is a ridiculously misconceived retaliation.

These Mayfair Boys were, after all, no more than young and extremely foolish amateurs. But what of Al Capone and 'Lucky' Luciano? What of the Great Train Robbers? Once again I could have selected other examples of these types of criminal who, though widely different in character and operation, possess certain features in common.

First, they are not by any ordinarily accepted standard to be considered mentally unbalanced; as often as not they make model family men. Secondly, they are strictly professionals—wholly committed to their way of life; if they quit it they should be regarded as retired rather than reformed, prison being for them usually just an occupational hazard and in some instances a hazard that is never realized. Finally, such punishment as I have outlined would plainly be useless in their case. Accordingly, *if* they were re-convicted of a serious crime, or convicted of a crime of violence, they would have to be deprived of their liberty.

That 'if' is important because, as I point out in the chapter on organized crime, Al Capone was never convicted of anything worse than income tax evasion, and clearly was sent to prison for eleven years by a federal court only because of his very unsavoury local reputation. 'Bugsy' Siegel, though rumoured to be guilty of almost as many murders and other serious crimes as Al Capone, was never in fact convicted of any of them. Whoever's fault this was—or whatever the deficiencies of the law enforcement system in various American jurisdictions—I could not possibly recommend that anyone be indefinitely deprived of his liberty on the basis of mere suspicion, however well founded that suspicion might be. His crimes would first of all have to be proved against him in a court of law, and the crimes so proved would have to be serious enough to justify loss of liberty. At the same time there would no longer be any question of 'copping a plea' or getting a lighter sentence in exchange for a plea of guilty. The choice that the court would have to make would be between punishment and deprivation of liberty.

Joseph Redenbaugh, who spent forty-five years in prison for murder, reformed himself. He remarked, shortly before his release, that doing time for him had been easy. 'It's like the monks,' he said. 'They have God; I had mathematics.' It wasn't in fact quite as easy for him as that. As he now sees it, he had to destroy his faith in crime and abandon his deep-rooted loyalties to the criminal world. Then he had to re-direct his skills and resources into constructive channels. It didn't take him anything approaching forty-five years to achieve this twofold task, but he wasn't completely sure of himself after twenty, and he knows that he could have succeeded far sooner than he did if he'd received realistic help or encouragement from those in authority over him.

Redenbaugh's self-reform indicates precisely what the objectives of custodial treatment should be, or rather, should have been, in the case of all the other professional criminals with whom I deal in this book, including the robbers and the confidence man (Lustig) as well as Luciano, Capone, Siegel and the rest referred to in my treatment of organized crime in America. Precisely how these objectives may be achieved would require far more knowledge than is possessed at present, but once the concept of punitive imprisonment is abandoned the search for answers may begin in earnest. The old adage 'set a thief to catch a thief' might be found to have a new relevance, for very possibly the person best equipped to reform the professional criminal is the ex-professional criminal who has *been* reformed or, like Redenbaugh, has reformed himself. What appears certain is that whoever is entrusted with the job of trying to influence professional criminals should be able to speak to them in their own language and, more than this, to be on their side—or at least to be able to *see* their point of view rather than automatically adopt a lofty attitude of disapproval.

Deprivation of liberty for the professional criminal would need (at any rate in its initial stages) to be especially secure, but this should not be a pretext for any punitive practices behind the perimeter. On the contrary, I suspect that in some cases it might be helpful to make the conditions of confinement as luxurious as possible—to make 'coddling' a planned part of treatment policy. The train robbers, for example, or most of them, had already proved themselves undeterred by imprisonment. They had exercised a free choice in favour of banditry, and were not so much rebels without a cause as rebels with a bad cause. In their case it might even have been worth testing the deterrent effectiveness of reward, the antithesis of punishment, which to a certain extent has been tried in, in fact forced on, prisons for the past 150 years and more. I am thinking of a very small custodial institution with a secure perimeter and a highly paternalistic regime. As in prison, the robbers would be relieved of all responsibilities. But at the same time they would be glutted with virtually every material comfort that they had aspired to obtain through crime.

The aim, of course, would be to make them realize for themselves the paramount value of the one thing that crime had cost them and that had become utterly unobtainable by them unless and until they were prepared to renounce crime, namely their freedom. I realize how profoundly shocking it may seem to suggest that the train robbers should have been 'rewarded' for stealing two and a half million pounds. I can produce no evidence in support of its practicability or likely effectiveness, because, so far as I'm aware, nothing quite like it has ever been tried. It may, however, be worth recalling a remark made by a committed criminal to Tony Parker, some years ago, during a recorded interview. The man in question had served several prison terms. He said he had no intention of ever abandoning crime. He said he had used violence, and would continue to use violence in a calculated way, when it was necessary to achieve an end, but not otherwise. He was asked whether he feared prison, and he said no. He was asked whether there was anything he feared, and he said there was only one thing and that was kindness.

I have no idea whether or not the train robbers feared kindness, though I am certain that they didn't expect it. Now that most of them have been paroled, it is possible that they have finally abandoned their commitment to crime. But if so, this has less than nothing to do with their prison 'training and treatment'.

For punitive imprisonment is, by its very nature, without reformative value. Anyone concerned about the prevention of crime should be looking for alternatives, and should be happy to find them.

Giles Playfair
December 1976

THE CHICAGO DAILY NEWS
BLUE STREAK
FINAL EDITION
THREE CENTS
THURSDAY, FEBRUARY 14, 1929.—FORTY-EIGHT PAGES.
MASSACRE 7 OF MORAN GANG
KILLING SCENE TOO GRUESOME FOR ONLOOKERS
View of Carnage Proves a Strain on Their Nerves.
IS LIKE A SHAMBLES
VICTIMS ARE LINED AGAINST WALL; ONE VOLLEY KILLS ALL
Assassins Pose as Policemen; Flee in "Squad Car" After Fusillade; Capone Revenge for Murder of Lombardo, Officers Believe.
Seven Moran-O'Banion gangsters were lined up against
the wall of a beer-distributing point at 2122 North Clark street
at 10:30 o'clock today. Four men, two of them in police uni-
forms, stood before them, armed with machine guns and sawed-
off shot guns. The leader of the execution squad barked an
order and the seven fell, six dying at once, the seventh three
hours later.
The execution, carried out with the precision of a Mexican
firing squad, is charged by the police to the Capone-Lombardo
interests. Greatest in point of numbers, it was also the most
cold-blooded in the history of Chicago's gangland slaughters.
The dead, as identified by the police, were:
GUSENBERG, PETER, notorious gunman for the O'Ban-
ion-Weiss-Drucci-Moran mob.
GUSENBERG, FRANK, brother of Peter. He died after
the others were killed, but refused to talk, though conscious.
WEINSHANK, AL, north side "alky" peddler.
MAY, JOHN, 1249 West Madison street, a $50-a-we
mechanic, apparently killed to silence him.
CLARK, JOHN, brother-in-law of George ("Bugs") M
ran, leader of the gang.
DAVIS, ARTHUR, west side racketeer.
FOSTER, FRANK, hoodlum.
Russell Opens War on Gangs

Left: Al Capone at the zenith of his power

Below left: *The Chicago Daily News,* 14 February 1929. One of the more famous crimes alleged against Al Capone but never proved

PART I
ORGANIZED CRIME

1/The American Version: Al Capone, 'Lucky' Luciano, Ben 'Bugsy' Siegel, Virginia Hill and others

Far too much has been written about organized crime in America, because far too much of it has been guessed at or imagined.

John Kobler's biography of the notorious Chicago gangster Al Capone was published in 1971. It is a long and apparently well researched book, and it begins (or almost begins) with a description of an event that allegedly took place on 7 May 1929 and has been the inspiration of scenes in a number of movies. Al gave a banquet at the Hawthorne Inn in Chicago, 'which to all practical purposes he owned', in honour of three Sicilians, who he knew, though they didn't know that he knew, had betrayed him. Throughout the meal, at which they ate and drank prodigiously, he was their genial host, but at the end of it, with the help of a baseball bat, he became their killer. His bodyguards bound them to their chairs and Al used the bat on each of them in turn with all his might, 'breaking bones in . . . shoulders, arms and chest' until they were reduced to 'mangled flesh and bone'. One of the bodyguards then went to rescue his revolver from the checkroom, where all revolvers had been checked in before the feast began, and shot each man in the back of the head, presumably in case Al's baseball bat hadn't quite done the trick.

There is, of course, no first-hand source given for this story, nor source of any kind other than its having been told, though with minor variations, by crime reporters and others before the author wrote his book. The story is in fact an important, perhaps the most important, part of the Capone legend, and also provides the chief grounds for branding him killer. According to Frederick Sondern, writing in 1959, 'the whole underworld and the Chicago police knew within hours what had happened'.[3]

But how could they really know? It is surely not as surprising or shocking as Mr Sondern seems to imagine that an indictment for murder was neither brought nor even sought against Capone. After all, no bodies were ever come upon in the banqueting hall at the Hawthorne Inn or any other banqueting hall in Chicago. No baseball bat, clean or bloodstained, was ever found near the alleged scene of the crime. True, the badly mauled bodies of three notorious Sicilians—John Scalise, Albert Anselmi and Guiseppi Giunta—were later discovered in a ditch near Hammond, Indiana. But no informer or witness of the crime came forward to say how or where the men had met their deaths or who was responsible. Nor can Mr Sondern reasonably consider this a matter for any wonderment, for he has also written in connection with the Capone gang that 'no informer could be bought, and it was impossible to infiltrate the brotherhood'.

Capone himself, of course, never acknowledged responsibility for the numerous gang murders that took place during his reign. Proof or convincing evidence that he was responsible for any of them does not exist; on the contrary, he told newspaper reporters that he could stop them. He was twice sent to prison: the first time in Philadelphia for carrying a revolver; the second and last time for the federal offence of income tax evasion. In both these cases, his reputation undoubtedly had everything to do with the severity of the sentence he received; eleven years largely served in Alcatraz, a prison designed for some six hundred of the most dangerous criminals in America, would hardly seem the appropriate punishment for so comparatively harmless an offence as tax evasion. Nevertheless, that was the worst that he was ever convicted of. And, therefore, to take one example, Mr Justice Lawton, who presided at the 'torture' trial of the English Richardson gang, though he was being understandably human, was hardly being suitably judicial when he took the opportunity in his sentencing speech to inform the defendants that their crimes reminded him of Al Capone.

Again, there is, and can be, no source for the frequently repeated story that 'Lucky' Luciano arranged for the murder of his boss Joe Masseria in 1931. It is true that some thirty years later, in 1963, Joe Valachi, a self-confessed murderer who gave a great deal of evidence before Senator McClellan's Committee, seemed to confirm this story, though even if his evidence had been available at the time it would never have stood up in a court of law; it would have been properly dismissed as so much hearsay. Luciano is supposed to have tricked Masseria into having a long and expensive lunch with him at Scarpato's in Coney Island. By three-thirty, they were the only customers left in the restaurant, and Luciano then visited the lavatory. While he was there he heard gunfire; he dashed back, and found that Masseria had been shot to death by some unknown persons who had entered the restaurant during his absence. This was the story Luciano told the police, and which the police quite rightly accepted. Unless Masseria's actual assailants had been found, which they never were, and had confessed that they were employed by Luciano, which it follows they did not, it is impossible to see how it could be proved, or for that matter fairly suggested, that Luciano was implicated. But the story was in print long before Joe Valachi had ever been heard of.

Joe Valachi was not the first but the second insider to make a full disclosure of the secrets of organized crime. The first was Abe 'Kid Twist' Reles, who preceded Valachi by nearly thirty years. Like Valachi he was a self-confessed murderer and was said to have total recall. Eventually, he either jumped or was pushed to his death from a window (it has never been decided which), but before that he proved a very voluble informant; and as a result of the information he had supplied, Burton B. Turkus, the New York assistant district attorney, was able to claim in *Murder Inc.*[4] that 'as a factor in national crime . . . the Mafia had been virtually extinct for two decades . . . Mafia was a closed corporation, demanding the scratched wrist, blood-brother initiation and the dread code of *Omerta*'. The Mafia, Turkus went on, had been replaced by a nationwide crime syndicate, which was the result of a peaceful alliance among leading mobsters of various ethnic groups; and the leading members of this syndicate, he said, each with his separate speciality, were Frank Costello, Lucky Luciano, Joe Adonis, Louis 'Lepke' Buchalter, 'Bugsy' Siegel, Meyer Lansky, Abner Zwillman, and 'Dutch' Schultz. Turkus was writing, of course, of the period Reles knew and talked of, namely

Below: Louis 'Lepke' Buchalter, the only major American gangster to have been executed

Bottom: Joe Valachi giving his information before the McClellan Committee in 1963

Opposite: An earlier informer, Abe Reles, either jumped or was pushed to his death from the sixth floor of a Coney Island hotel

DINE & DANCE
KOPPER
OCEAN TERRACE
BANQUET ACCOMMODATIONS
10 TO 1000
MENUS ON REQUEST

the thirties. By the time his book was published Lucky Luciano had been deported to Italy after serving a prison sentence for exploiting prostitution, while Siegel and Schultz had been murdered and Buchalter had been executed.

But Valachi in the course of his evidence before the McClellan Committee in 1963 also spoke of the period that Reles had known, and his account of it was very different. He belonged, he said, not to the Mafia, a name never used in his experience, but to an all-Italian secret society called La Cosa Nostra. He had been initiated into La Cosa Nostra at a ceremony which included blood-letting. That was in 1930, when Joseph Marrazano was in charge, and Joseph Bonanno acted as his sponsor. Marrazano was murdered shortly afterwards, again, according to the crime reporters, on Luciano's orders, and Valachi then transferred his loyalty to Luciano, who was succeeded after his deportation at first by Costello and then by Vito Genovese. Valachi described the organization of La Cosa Nostra in detail. It consisted of all-Italian families throughout the nation, each with its own boss or 'Don', its captain, lieutenant and soldiers. At any one time between nine and twelve of the most important bosses constituted the 'commission' or ruling body, which settled or attempted to settle disputes between families or revolts within families, acted as a kangaroo court, and laid down general policy rules, though it tried to refrain from interfering in the affairs of individual families.

According to his story Valachi had never risen above the status of soldier in all his thirty years of membership of La Cosa Nostra. *Omerta*—or an abridged version of it—was made clear to him on his initiation: to betray La Cosa Nostra secrets, or to violate the wife of any member, would mean death without trial. It is hard to see what advantages he derived from belonging to La Cosa Nostra, at least with so lowly a status. He was required to commit, or help to commit, a number of murders, but he was never paid for doing so. Nor did his 'family' finance him in any way or suggest illicit activities from which he might profit (he had to think these up for himself) or provide him with protection in the form of legal help and bail on those occasions when he was picked up.

Abe Reles, on the other hand, was (according to his information) one of several men, all apparently Brooklyn born, who for a fee would accept a 'contract' to go anywhere to 'hit' (kill) anyone whom the syndicate wished to be rid of. They were servants of the syndicate, just as

Valachi was a common soldier in La Cosa Nostra, but unlike him they were paid, and paid well, for doing their dirty work, and they became known to the press as Murder Incorporated. Turkus tells how two of them, Joseph Schaffer and George Young, were contracted to 'hit' a gangster named Wagner, who had caused the syndicate displeasure, and finally caught up with him in the Midway Restaurant between Minneapolis and St Paul. But they were apprehended before they left the state. 'The immediate concern', writes Turkus, 'was to keep them from the chair . . . A fortune was spent and the pair did escape the chair.' That particular statement is demonstrably false, since—and it is surprising that an assistant district attorney should have been unaware of this—capital punishment had been abolished years before in Minnesota. Nevertheless it can be said, on the strength of the word of one of its most trusted former inmates, that Schaffer and Young received exceptionally benevolent treatment while they were serving their life sentences at Stillwater penitentiary.

Reles's information, moreover, led to the conviction for murder and subsequent execution of several of his associates and also of one of the alleged members of the nationwide syndicate, Louis 'Lepke' Buchalter, described by J. Edgar Hoover in 1939 as 'the most dangerous criminal in the United States'. Buchalter arranged for the killing of a man who had proved himself a minor hindrance to his extortion racket in the New York garment district. His execution was stayed for twenty-four hours—it eventually took place on 4 March 1944—by order of Governor Thomas E. Dewey. Apparently Buchalter had agreed to provide the government with important information, but whatever that may have been it didn't prove enough to save him. After his death, his wife read a statement from him which said that he had refused to 'speak of the national cartel'.

This may have been due to Buchalter's deep respect for the German-Jewish equivalent of *Omerta,* or simply to his inability to give details about something of which he knew nothing. Whichever the case, his silence has proved unhelpful in trying to decide whether organized crime in America is controlled by a national syndicate made up of various ethnic groups, or by an all-Italian body which has come to be known interchangeably as the Mafia or La Cosa Nostra, or whether in the sense of its being directed nationally by a dominant group organized crime does not exist at all.

Certain things, however, are undisputed. Al Capone

Opposite: 'Dutch' Schultz, murdered in a New York restaurant in 1935

may or may not have been innocent of killing anyone, but during his period in Chicago in the twenties and early thirties murders and gun-battles took place on an unprecedented scale. Nor has the peace which Johnnie Torrio, Capone's great friend and benefactor, is supposed to have suggested to a receptive Luciano ever proved completely effective—even in New York where Luciano operated before his imprisonment. Thus Dutch Schultz, named by Turkus as one of New York's chief gangsters, was murdered in 1935; and in 1957 Albert Anastasia, reputedly the boss of a Mafia or Cosa Nostra 'family', was gunned to death while sitting in a barber's chair at the Waldorf Astoria. Their assailants, of course, were never identified.

Frederick Sondern has described Al Capone as 'unquestionably the greatest organizer of crime in his or any other era'. The Internal Revenue investigations revealed that he had undoubtedly earned a great deal of money from his life in the rackets: that is, from supplying illicit goods and services, which, for him, proved an exceptionally easy and profitable task because of Prohibition. But gang chieftains in the post-Prohibition era, both those of Italian origin and those of other ethnic origins, all seem to have accumulated, and kept, considerable wealth.

Whether or not they eventually landed in prison—and some of them like Capone were convicted of nothing worse than tax evasion—it is clear that they could never have provided the illicit goods and services which they did provide without political cooperation. The Wickersham Commission reported to President Hoover in 1931: 'The presence of any significant organized crime in America necessarily means local criminal justice has been corrupted to some degree.' That was putting it too mildly. For instance, in 1928, Frank Loesch, president of the Chicago Crime Commission, was obliged to approach Capone in order to get a guarantee of a free election. For he had been convinced that Capone controlled the police, and he was satisfied from the result of Capone's intervention that he was right. It was 'the squarest and most successful election day in forty years', he said later in a lecture. Nor is there any doubt that gangsters such as Luciano, Adonis and Costello intervened with their money and hence their influence in New York politics. In fact, as Professor Daniel Bell has pointed out,[5] Adonis made a sizeable contribution to Mayor La Guardia's initial campaign, though La Guardia later became the sworn enemy of racketeers and racketeering.

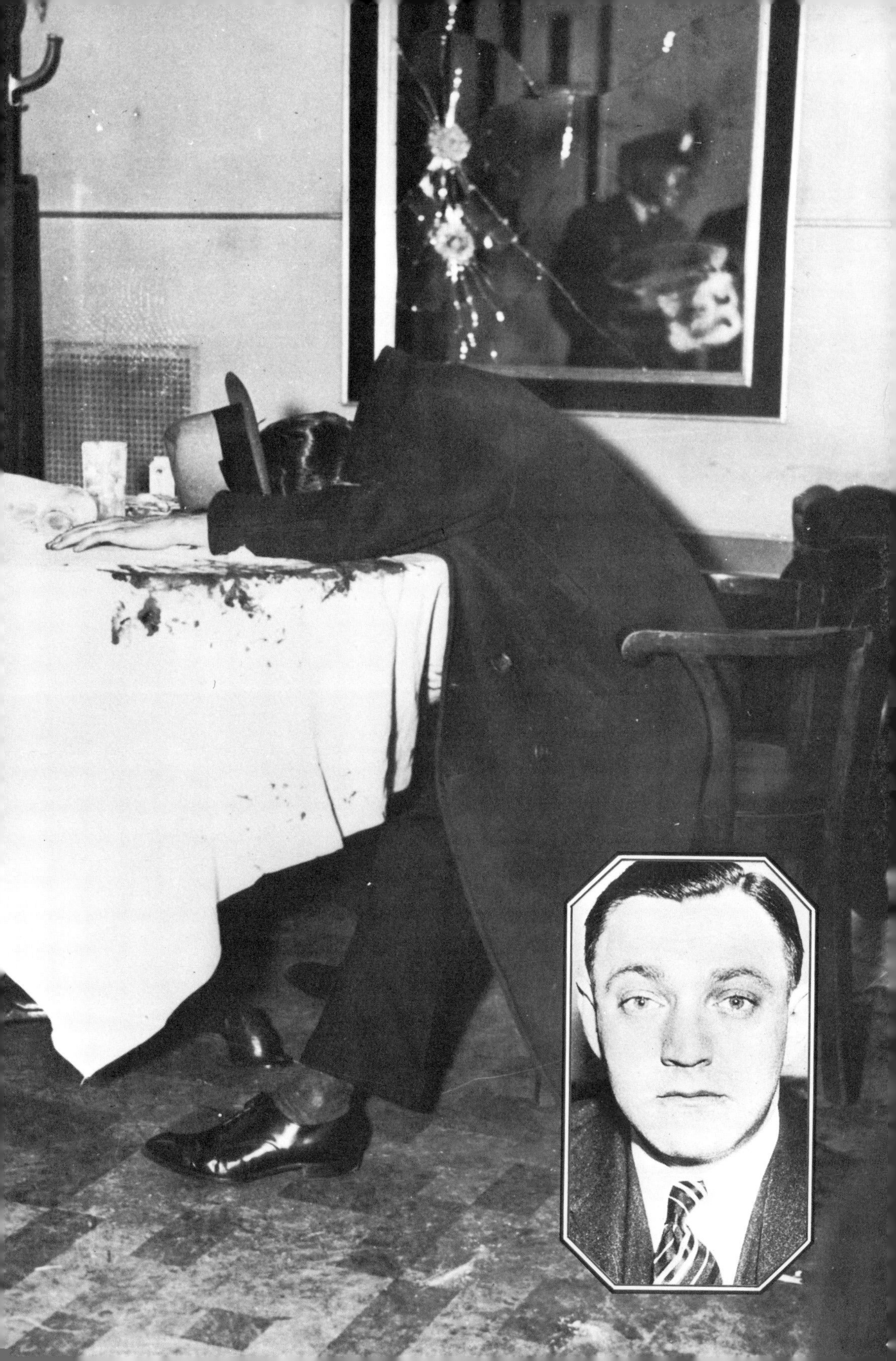

Below and right: Albert Anastasia who was gunned to death in a barber's chair in 1947

Below right: Charles 'Lucky' Luciano

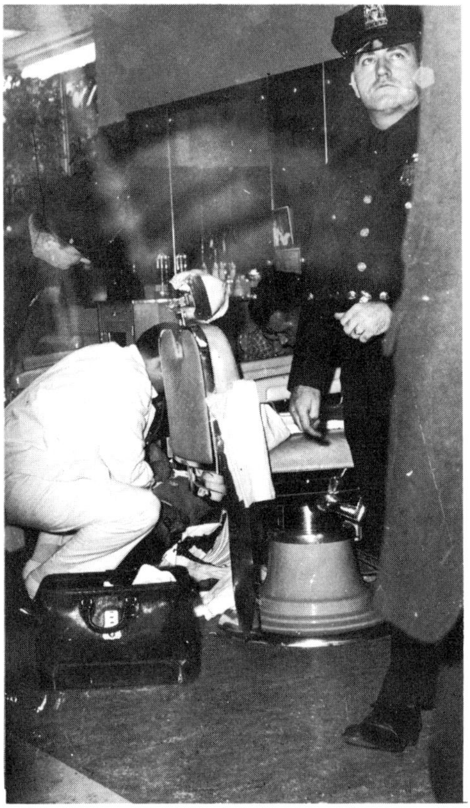

In a brilliantly argued chapter from their book *The Honest Politician's Guide to Crime Control*[6] Norval Morris and Gordon Hawkins go further than anyone else in dismissing as myth 'the notion that behind the diverse phenomena of crime there exists a single, mysterious omnipotent organization which is responsible for much of it'. And they conclude that the way to 'eliminate organized crime is to remove the criminal laws which both stimulate and protect it', by which they mean the laws, for example, that make the use of narcotics a criminal offence. It would certainly seem likely that if anyone were permitted to obtain any drug, including heroin, on prescription from a licensed chemist, this would largely put a stop to the illicit traffic in narcotics, as the repeal of Prohibition put an end to the illicit traffic in alcohol. Moreover, gambling, which today provides organized crime with the bulk of its income, is illegal in one form or another throughout the jurisdictions of the United States, with the exception of Nevada. At the same time, it cannot be fairly argued that all the goods and services supplied by organized crime are legally forbidden ones which a significant part of the public are unprepared to do without. The extortion and protection rackets clearly do not come within such a definition. As one small instance of this, a movie theatre owner in Chicago was forced to pay $20,000 to a post-Capone gang—or his projectionist would have struck.

Professor Donald Cressey in his book *Theft of a Nation*[7] takes an extreme view precisely opposed to that of Morris and Hawkins. He is wholly persuaded that there is a commission or ruling body of La Cosa Nostra which wields immense power over most criminal activity in the country. He implies, furthermore, that it could, if it wished, veto major crime committed by criminals of non-Italian origin, but, in fact, 'still tolerates' this.

If that is true, it is hard to account for the murder of Anastasia, a reputed head of a 'family' and member of the commission. Two reasons have been advanced for this, neither of them at all convincing if the commission were really all-powerful and concerned to put an end to gang warfare. Frederick Sondern believes that Anastasia was punished for sending his agents into Cuba without the local boss's permission. Joseph Valachi, on the other hand, as quoted by Peter Maas in *The Valachi Papers*,[8] asserts that the murder of Anastasia was organized by Vito Genovese in the belief that Anastasia was 'meeting secretly' with Frank Costello, whom Genovese planned to supplant as boss of his own 'family'. A little while before an attempt had been made on Costello's life, for which Valachi claimed that Genovese was also responsible. In short Valachi was saying that the commission, far from being able to enforce peace, was unable to keep peace among its own members.

While Gay Talese in his book *Honor Thy Father*[9] has no doubt that a commission of what he prefers to call the Mafia (rather than La Cosa Nostra) exists, he says that the Mafia itself is merely a small part of the organized crime industry. His book is described as 'a family portrait', for it is written with the full approval and cooperation of Salvatore (Bill) Bonanno, son and devoted follower of Joseph Bonanno, who was supposedly a member of the commission up to the time he was kidnapped in 1964. One learns from this book that in spite of the fact that Mafia members are in legitimate business, and the younger generation among them well educated, they go around armed and try to settle disputes within a 'family' by the bullet. But unfortunately, although this is a very long book (over 500 pages), with intimate details of Bill Bonanno's family life, one is told next to nothing about the secrets of the Mafia that has not already been told or alleged. Nor is anything said that could possibly cause Bill's father the least harm from the law or anyone else. No explanation is offered of why or by whom he was kidnapped or what happened to him during the eighteen months before his sudden reappearance in a New York courtroom. In the context of Mr Talese's book, one would have thought this a virtual *scène à faire,* but evidently Bill's cooperation did not go far enough to enable him to produce it.

Much of what has been written about organized crime in America is apparently sourceless allegation; and a lot of it is contradictory. For example, there are three different versions of how Luciano came to be nicknamed 'Lucky'. The first, and most dramatic, is that as a very young, but nonetheless already prominent, gangster, he was 'taken for a ride', horribly battered about, hung up by his fingernails, and considered amazingly fortunate to have lived to tell the tale. The second, and more mundane, is that he was extraordinarily lucky at cards—he is supposed to have played cards with Masseria before taking his famous trip to the lavatory. The third, and most likely, has a named source—Luciano himself. In 1954, he was interviewed by William Safire, who was then in Naples as an army corporal assigned to the American Forces Network in Europe. Safire describes Luciano as 'a cautious, polite, swarthy gentleman', who at first was reluctant to speak into a microphone, but eventually agreed to. Safire asked him how he got his nickname: '"Bein' that my right name was Luccania", he said matter-of-factly, "it was cut short when I was a young boy, and made it Lucky."'[10]

Of course, it may be argued that Luciano was not a particularly reliable source about himself,* and presumably he wasn't in the sense that he denied even the prostitution charges that had been proved against him. Still, one is inclined to prefer a story with a source, however unreliable, to one with no source at all; and in this case Luciano could hardly have had a reason to lie.

Possibly the most glaring contradictions concern the murder of Ben Siegel in 1947. Siegel was German-Jewish, and extraordinarily handsome. He was not, at least to look at, a 'vulgar, cigar-waving thug, like Al Capone', to quote Dean Jennings, who has written a biography of him comparatively recently;[12] and that in itself distinguishes him from other famous racketeers of yesterday and today. Siegel's murder, which was never solved, caused a considerable sensation simply because he was so notorious. He was peppered with bullets as he sat in the living room of a palatial house that belonged to a woman named Virginia Hill, to whom he was secretly married. The gunman shot him through an open window.

Turkus, who maintained that Siegel was a member of the governing body of organized crime (the 'syndicate'), also claimed that it was a syndicate decision to send Siegel to California in 1937. '"Benny is a natural", proposed Lepke, "he knows the angles. And since we got the Brooklyn troup to handle the contracts, Ben is loose to take care of big stuff like this."'[13] Decorative dialogue of that sort, incidentally, is typical of virtually all books about American organized crime, excepting those written by criminologists. The further removed in time these books are from the age of permissiveness, the more unreal the decorative dialogue is likely to seem by comparison with the transcripts of tapped or bugged conversations between gangsters, which seem to contain a 'fuck' or a 'shit' in every sentence.

* There has now appeared a book (a huge bestseller in America) called *The Last Testament of Lucky Luciano* by Martin Gosch and Richard Hammer[11] in which, as may be guessed, Luciano is alleged to be the completely reliable source of all the information about him. This includes the story that William Safire none the less learned from the same source was untrue, and indeed some of the provenly inaccurate stories told by crime reporters. It also includes anachronisms (Lucky's views on things that happened after his death) and unsubstantiated allegations against public figures. It may safely be dismissed as unreliable.

NUGGET
ALL
PIONEER
SALOON
STATE
LOANS
MIKE'S
Club
SAVOY
BOULDER
CLUB
Eldorado

Turkus said, too, that before his departure for California Siegel, together with Meyer Lansky, was responsible for 'enforcement'; and in this Virgil Peterson, operating director of the Chicago Crime Commission and former F.B.I. agent, agreed in his testimony to the Kefauver Committee of 1950, except that he added the name of Luciano to those of Siegel and Lansky and said that all three comprised the enforcement branch of the 'Costello organization'. Costello, rather than Luciano, was considered by the Kefauver Committee itself as the top man of the Mafia, while Vito Genovese, though back in the United States after having fled to Italy from a murder charge before the war, was hardly mentioned.

Opposite: Las Vegas in the early forties and (below) George Raft with his arm round Ben 'Bugsy' Siegel

Understandably, perhaps, Turkus assumed, though in this he could have had no information from Abe Reles who was already long since dead, that Siegel was 'hit' on orders from the syndicate. The syndicate's decision was taken, according to him and others who have told more or less the same story, in Havana, Cuba, where Luciano had arrived from Italy and where the leaders of organized crime, including Siegel himself, had come to meet him. The thing that finally decided the syndicate to eliminate Siegel was his determination to hang on to the Trans-America Race Wire Service in California and Nevada when the Chicago outfit had won control of the Continental Wire Service.

Dean Jennings, however, cannot decide why or on whose orders Siegel was 'hit', since he departs completely from Turkus's premise. For one thing, he denies that Siegel's coming to California had anything to do with the syndicate; it was entirely his own decision made for his own reasons. Further, Jennings says that Siegel did not go to Havana to meet Luciano, although one must add—it is an illustration of the contradictoriness of the available literature—that Ed Reid and Ovid Demaris in *The Green Felt Jungle*[14] give the most vivid account of Siegel's meeting with Luciano in a Havana hotel, including decorative dialogue. They also assert that 'with the assistance of Dragna [said to be the number one mafioso in the district, but presumably subordinate to Siegel] he set up a narcotics pipeline through Mexico to import dope from all over the world. A brigade of smugglers was organized with Joe Sica at the receiving end. A rotation system was established to handle prostitutes from Seattle to San Diego.'

Jennings, while acknowledging Siegel's close association with Dragna as well as with other racketeers, doesn't believe that he ever had anything to do with narcotics or prostitution. And Jennings does at least name sources for most of his statements. These sources cannot all necessarily be accepted as reliable. Mickey Cohen, for instance, a self-confessed ex-thief and strong-arm man—a 'punk', he himself said that he had been—was serving a long sentence for tax evasion when Jennings interviewed him in the penitentiary. Nevertheless, what Jennings says about Siegel seems a good deal more likely than previously written stories. Broadly speaking it is this: that though Siegel never really tried to get out of the rackets, he came to Los Angeles with the object of winning acceptance for himself as a wealthy sportsman. And to an extent he plainly succeeded. J. Edgar Hoover commented after his death: 'The circumstances surrounding Bugsy Siegel's career in crime tell the story better than words. Here was an individual whose life was a constant challenge to common decency. Yet he and his criminal scum were lionised and their favours sought after in so-called respectable circles.'[15]

Siegel was just over 30 when he finally settled in Los Angeles, and he must have possessed considerable charm as well as good looks. He was also remarkably vain; and George Raft, his childhood friend, who had come up in his different way from the same New York slum, learned to call him 'Baby Blue Eyes' when he found it necessary to melt his sometimes terrifying anger. Siegel had no record of convictions either as a killer or a gangster, but it was generally accepted that he was both, and Hollywood stars and other non-criminals either fraternized with him in spite of this knowledge or avoided him because of it. In 1939, he was arrested and charged with the murder of 'Big Greenie' Greenberg, a man who (so it was said) had once been used by Buchalter for strike breaking and as an expert on stink bombs, but had latterly turned up in Los Angeles and made a nuisance of himself with his demands for money. It is almost certain that Abe Reles and Allie Tannenbaum, who had also turned informant for Turkus, could have provided the evidence to convict Siegel of this 'contract' murder in which he actually participated. But William O'Dwyer, the New York district attorney, insisted that these two key witnesses were needed in New York and couldn't be allowed to travel to California. The case against Siegel had to be dismissed for lack of evidence, and he was released from the county gaol.

But for all that, one senses a kind of naivety about Siegel, a genuine desire to become the wealthy sportsman he said he was. If he was no 'cigar-waving thug' like

Capone, neither did he possess Capone's powers of organization. He could be extremely rough-tongued as well as rough, especially when anyone called him 'Bugsy', a nickname which, possibly because it reminded him of his past, he detested. On the other hand, some of his enterprises were perfectly legitimate, and appeared to be more the extravagant result of a child's dreaming than a racketeer's ruthlessness. For example, there was the treasure hunt: he placed complete trust in a man who showed him an ancient map, and on the strength of this chartered a yacht and crew to take him to the island where the treasure was supposedly buried. The Countess di Frasso, an American millionairess with an Italian husband, joined him in this venture, which inevitably came to nothing. Later he went to Italy with the Countess, who was apparently his mistress—or rather was one among several.

Moreover, evidently it was the romanticism in him that inspired his last disastrous enterprise. This was to transform what was then a desert near Las Vegas, Nevada, into a vast, highly ornate hotel-casino, which he named the Flamingo. True, the other shareholders in the Flamingo, where Siegel had his own suite of rooms (he had sold his house in Los Angeles), were mostly ex-criminals, but the gambling was conducted honestly, as of course it had to be in the circumstances, and Siegel's chief employees were perfectly respectable people. The construction of this dream palace entailed a huge outlay, for Siegel would spare no expense on it, and there wasn't any immediate return; on the contrary there were heavy losses, and the continuing worry, for as long as Siegel lived, of whether and how he could keep afloat. He declined the offer of a $50,000 loan from the Countess—the one thing Jennings holds to his credit—but at the time of his death he still owed $100,000 to George Raft. His failure with the Flamingo may well have accounted for the fact that he was 'hit'. At any rate, the place began to make money almost as soon as he was out of the way—and not under notably less crime-tainted direction.

Siegel, like the great majority of American gangsters, was born in poverty, but no other member of his large family was criminal, and his brother became a successful physician. According to Jennings, he once told Del Webb, his building contractor, that he had killed twelve men in his time, but then added with a laugh, 'there's no chance that you'll get killed, we only kill each other'. That may have been the truth, though the reasons given for unsolved gang or 'contract' murders, even if there was never any attempt made to put an end to them, would often seem merely frivolous, and Siegel does not appear to have been a man who enjoyed killing for killing's sake.

Neither, obviously, did Buchalter, who never smeared his own hands with one murder. He was remarkably gentle in manner and soft-spoken, and though he came from as poor a background as Siegel he had a brother who became a clergyman. In other words, it is impossible to explain either Buchalter or Siegel in terms of childhood poverty or psychopathy, and no such explanation can account for the existence of organized crime in America and the murders associated with it, although some of the men who actually 'hit' were undoubtedly psychopathic.

It may be that vanity had a great deal to do with Siegel's criminal career, and, as we shall see, vanity is a failing common to most criminals of whatever kind; vanity, that is, combined with an absence of conscience. But, in his case, vanity also urged him to renounce crime, or to pretend that he had, and he sent his two daughters by his first wife to a private boarding school.

On the other hand, his second wife Virginia Hill, whom he married secretly, was, to judge from her speech, what one would consider a gross caricature of a gangster's moll if portrayed by an actress. She was born in Alabama, one of ten children, and at a very young age she went to Chicago, where she met a rich bookmaker named Joe Epstein, with whom she lived for a while then and spasmodically afterwards. For some extraordinary reason which has never been satisfactorily explained, Epstein sent her huge sums of money in cash whenever she asked for it, whether she was in New York, California or where-have-you. She was extremely pretty in her youth, but violent, neurotic, and vulgar. She attacked and badly injured a girl at the Flamingo who she supposed had designs on Siegel, though she herself reputedly had innumerable lovers before, during and after the time she was with him. Then she made the first of several suicide attempts by swallowing sleeping pills, and had to be rushed to hospital by Siegel. Shortly afterwards she took herself off to Paris, and was there at the time he was murdered. That news led to her second suicide attempt.

In 1950 she married a German ski-instructor named Hans Hoover, and by him she gave birth to a son. But, according to Jennings, she had not forgotten and never would forget Ben. On one occasion, when she was being interviewed by reporters, she produced an old, crumpled piece of paper from her handbag and started to read from it, saying it was a poem Ben had written to her. But then she thought better of it. 'Oh, the hell with it. You bums wouldn't get it anyway.' Jennings also says that her favourite book was one called *Forever* by Mildred Cram, because it ended with the words, 'Julie lifted her head. "This is forever," she said.' That was enough to convince her she'd see Ben again.

She already looked much older than her age—she was just over 30—in March 1951, when she was called to give evidence before the Kefauver Committee, which was conducting its investigation into organized crime. But she could still be most entertainingly brash. She was asked what she knew of a certain reputed gangster (she was suspected of being the friend of every important gangster in the country), and she replied simply,'He's a louse.' And when she was questioned about Joe Epstein, she was marvellously evasive. She said that if she wanted to reach him she could call the Clover Club in Chicago, and ask if he 'was around'. But doesn't Joe Epstein have a phone or a place of business? she was asked. 'Oh, he has some books. I used to see him working on books.'[16]

Most of her life after this was spent in Switzerland, hiding from the Internal Revenue, which had charged her with tax evasion. She was apparently never happy. She was a wrinkled old moll when at last, in 1967, she succeeded in killing herself aged 48. It is hard to believe that if she were really going to see Ben again he would have found her in any way a fitting adjunct to his vanity.

Virginia Hill, Siegel's second wife, on her way to testify before the Kefauver Committee in 1951

2/The British Imitation: The Kray Twins, the Mad Axeman and their associates

One may judge from Siegel's story that whether or not there is some supra-body in control of crime, or most of it, an American gangster can with relative impunity become far richer and wield far greater power than has up to now proved possible in Britain. Organized crime in America does not, after all, include such common offences as burglary, which engage the attention of ordinary police detection; these are left to the 'punks'. For what organized crime does include, it requires, as has been said, a high degree of political cooperation or corruption of justice on a local level. And by 'local' is meant everything except federal. Significantly, prominent gangsters such as Al Capone, Frank Costello and Joe Adonis only came to grief through evading federal taxes.

Nothing, at least on an equivalent scale, has happened in Britain as yet; nor had it happened before the legalization of gambling, which has succeeded bootlegging as the greatest money-spinner among illicit activities in the United States. Since Britain made gaming legal, a number of American visitors to London have been required to return to their homeland. They include Anthony Corallo, known to the press as 'Tony Ducks', a man with a fairly long criminal record, and George Raft (born Ranft), who has never ceased to be Siegel's admirer and apologist. But these facts would seem to confirm, rather than deny, that there has been no corruption of justice in Britain, and that, therefore, organized crime on the American model cannot and does not exist.

But the Kray twins with their 'Firm', their murders, and their foray from the East End into the West End of London gave an effect of being the exact equivalent of the big American racketeers; and when they were finally convicted in 1969 and sentenced to life imprisonment (with a recommendation that they should serve thirty years), it was commonly imagined that these two men, brought down by the determined persistence of the police, had once been as rich and powerful as any Siegel or Capone. Actually, they applied for and were granted legal aid; and the judge was informed at the end of their trial that a house in Suffolk, valued at £11,000 and anyway purchased in their mother's name, was the only substantial asset they had left.

Nevertheless, there were certain superficial resemblances between the Kray twins and the best-known leaders of organized crime in America. They were feared, though only because of their own capacity for violence. They made in their time comparatively large sums of money, though they kept very little of it. They subscribed,

Opposite left to right: Reggie, Charles and Ronnie Kray

1894
THE BLIND BEGGAR
MANNS
BEER
THE BLIND BEGGAR
MILE END GATE

with a considerable accompaniment of publicity, to a number of charities, though not, like Costello, Adonis, and Luciano, with discretion, to political campaigns. They liked to mix with the famous and socially respectable; and much of their business was legitimate. But it was an extraordinary achievement on their part to take over a fashionable gaming club in the West End called Esmeralda's Barn, which was rightly known as a goldmine, and end up by making a substantial loss!

Opposite: The Blind Beggar, where George Cornell was murdered by Ronnie Kray

Above left: The Richardson brothers, Charles and Eddie, for whom George Cornell (above) worked

Their life-style was a conscious imitation of the American gangster—or rather of their idea of him. They acted out a fantasy. Before they got any distance with this, while they were still no more than East End thugs, one of them, Ronnie, had been sent to prison for three years. While serving this sentence he was certified insane, and was controllable only by drugs at the time of his release. But Ronnie, apparently, always dominated his twin brother Reggie, who left to himself might have behaved less madly. Still both of them were clearly paranoid in the sense of being continually on the look-out for a slight, and making it the pretext for their kind of vengeance. This graduated from grievous bodily harm to murder. They were a good deal above averagely tough and strong.

The British are far more inhibited by the law of libel than the Americans, and even after the Kray twins had become well known as gangsters and killers, at least among the cognoscenti, no one would have dared to call them either until they had been proved to be both in a court of law. Since then, two full-length books have been written about them. One is by a professional writer, John Pearson, and was published in 1972.[17] The other came out in the following year, and is the work of an underworld character named Leslie Payne,[18] who at one time collaborated with or, more accurately, guided the Krays in some of their non-violent activities, though later he turned against them.

John Pearson relates in the introduction to his book that he was asked by the Krays seven months before their final arrest to write their 'official' biography, and agreed to undertake this task. He says that he saw them regularly thereafter, that they were good raconteurs with 'extraordinary memories' (like Abe Reles and Joe Valachi, both of whom, it will be remembered, were said to have 'total recall'!). Unfortunately, however, it is impossible to tell how much of the rest of Mr Pearson's book draws upon what the Krays confided to him, though one must suppose rather little. After all, their own explanation for wanting their biography written was that they planned to retire, and thought it time the 'true story' was told. It seems most unlikely that this 'true story' contained accounts of the murders and other criminal acts with which Mr Pearson deals at length.

Payne, a criminal, it seems, of unusual intelligence, was not a member of the Kray twins' 'Firm', as their gang was called. That consisted of thugs, mostly born and bred in the East End, and not all of them loyal to the last in the true spirit of *Omerta*. Payne, while he had little respect for either Kray's brainpower (unlike Pearson, who seems to have had quite a bit for Reggie's), evidently thought their capacity for spreading fear might be useful to him in his legitimate, fraudulent and semi-fraudulent ventures.

Payne's story of the murder of Cornell in the Blind Beggar public house differs somewhat from Pearson's regarding motive. According to Payne, the Krays had no intention of killing Cornell simply because he was working for another gang—the Richardsons. But a merchant had handed them £2,000 to get Cornell off his back, and Cornell, when they told him about this, declined to be scared off and said he would carry on regardless. This was a slight, an aspersion on the Krays' reputation, especially when the merchant started complaining about the quality of the protection the Krays offered. It meant they had to do something, and 'doing something', Ronnie decided, meant murder.

Pearson's story is more dramatic. A full-scale gang war had developed between the Krays and the Richardsons, which culminated in a gun battle at Mr Smith's Club on the London–Eastbourne Road at Catford. Though the twins were not involved in this, the Richardsons were, and it led immediately to their downfall. Cornell was the only important one among them still at large, and he had to die because an ally of the Krays, one Richard Hart, had been killed in the battle at Mr Smith's Club. Ronnie felt this 'personally'.

However, Payne and Pearson are agreed that there was a subsidiary motive: namely, that Cornell had called Ronnie 'a fat poof' behind his back. Ronnie didn't object to being called a homosexual. In fact, he was proud to be seen with good-looking boys, and resented his brother Reggie's heterosexuality. But to be called a 'poof', which implied effeminacy, was thoroughly objectionable.

There is no doubt according to the evidence given at the trial about how the murder was done. At 8.30 p.m. on 9 March 1966 Ronnie and Ian Barrie, a member of the Firm, were driven by Scotch Jack Dickson to the Blind Beggar. Ronnie and Barrie entered the saloon. They found Cornell sitting with two friends at the far end of the bar. Barrie fired two shots into the ceiling, as a warning of what was coming, and then Ronnie shot Cornell through the head.

The motive for the murder of McVitie is hardly commented on by Payne. Pearson supposes that it was ultimately because McVitie had appeared, very drunk, obviously without any awareness of what he was doing or saying, at the Regency Club one night, carrying a sawn-off shot gun. John Barry, the manager of the club, disarmed him, but someone told Ronnie the following day that McVitie had threatened to shoot both him and his brother.

So McVitie was tricked into attending a party where the twins and some members of the Firm were waiting for him. Reggie tried to shoot him in the head as he came in, but the gun jammed. McVitie dived for a window, but got stuck in the frame, and they pulled him back. Ronnie locked McVitie's arms behind his back, and Reggie was standing there with a carving knife in his hand. 'Kill him, Reg! Do him! Don't stop now,' said Ronnie, or words to that effect. It could be deduced from the evidence of Ronnie Hart, a member of the Firm and a cousin of the twins, that Ronnie Kray wanted Reggie to do a murder, so that they could be even. Reggie pushed the knife into McVitie's face below the eye. Ronnie Hart testified that Reggie then stabbed the man's stomach and chest and finally impaled him through the throat on the floor.

Next to nothing, it should be emphasized, was gained

10 DAILY SKETCH, Friday, January 10, 1969

Kray twins took

AN INVITATION JACK THE HAT

Jack McVitie . . . known as "The Hat"

George Cornell . . . died at the bar

PETER BURDEN: Chief Crime Reporter

THE story of a man's last moments of terror as he faced his murderer in a London flat was told to a jury at the Old Bailey yesterday.

The victim, said prosecuting counsel Mr. Kenneth Jones, QC, was Jack "The Hat" McVitie. And his murderer was Reginald Kray.

McVitie, who got his nickname because he almost invariably wore a hat to hide his baldness, had been lured to the flat on the promise of a party, said Mr. Jones.

In fact he had been invited to his own execution. Reginald Kray first tried to shoot him but the gun failed.

Mr. Jones went on: "McVitie was at last fully aware of what was to happen to him. This was no party. Terrified, bathed in sweat, like a caged animal he tried to escape by throwing himself at the window, smashing it as he did so."

Mr. Jones told the packed Number Two Court that the Kray twins, Ronald and Reginald, pulled McVitie back, aided by a man named Hart.

'Like a caged animal he threw

'DEADLY WORK WAS DONE'

Then, as Ronald Kray held McVitie's hands behind his back, Reginald stabbed him in the face with a knife. This was followed by Reginald punching McVitie over the heart—to stop the bleeding of the stabs to follow, the prosecution alleged.

Then, with Ronald Kray urging his twin "Kill him Reg" over and over again Reginald Kray stabbed McVitie.

Finally said Mr. Jones "Reginald Kray stood beside him, plunged the knife into his neck twice, twisting it to make sure its deadly work was done."

'FRESH CLOTHES FOR KRAYS'

During the knifing, he claimed, Reginald Kray cut his left hand—and still bore the scar.

Elaborate steps were then taken to clear up the room where McVitie had been killed, said Mr. Jones.

The weapons were thrown into the canal and fresh clothes were brought for the Kray twins and Hart.

Their old clothes were put into a suitcase and burned on a rubbish dump. The Kray twins also got rid of their watches, rings and paper money.

The job of disposing of the body, Mr. Jones alleged, was given to Frederick Foreman, licensee of the Prince of Wales, a public house in South London.

Why was McVitie murdered? Mr. Jones claimed that he was the victim selected by Reginald Kray to prove that he was the equal of his twin brother in violence and would kill too.

The Kray twins sat silently in the heavily guarded dock as the story was told.

With eight other men in the dock yesterday they face an indictment concerning allegations in relation to the killing of Jack McVitie and George Cornell.

'I'VE DONE MY ONE'

Cornell was shot dead in the Blind Beggar public house in Stepney, East London, in March, 1966. McVitie, a bookmaker's clerk, was killed in a flat in Stoke Newington in October 1967.

The ten accused are: Ronald Kray, aged 34 and his twin brother Reginald Kray, their elder brother

Daily Sketch, 10 January 1969

from either of these murders. They may be seen fundamentally as the acts of two madmen who, whether they realized it or not, were bent on self-destruction. On the other hand, it might be said of the Krays, as Siegel is supposed to have said of himself, that they 'only killed each other', and that left them a very limited choice. Undoubtedly they were remarkably successful engineers of terror, for the police had to get them under lock and turns to kill, claims Old Bailey prosecutor

TO DEATH . . . 'THE PARTY FOR ENDED WITH HIS EXECUTION'

The saloon bar of the Blind Beggar in Stepney. Here, according to the prosecution, Ronald Kray murdered George Cornell—and was recognised by the barmaid.

himself against the window'

Charles Kray, Cornelius Whitehead, Christopher Lambrianou, Anthony Lambrianou, Ronald Albert Bender, Anthony Barry, Frederick Foreman and John Barrie.

Ronald Kray, and John Barrie plead not guilty to the murder of George Cornell. Reginald Kray pleads not guilty to being an accessory after the fact to the murder of Cornell. The Kray twins, Christopher Lambrianou, Anthony Lambrianou, Bender, and Anthony Barry all plead not guilty to the murder of Jack McVitie. Charles Kray, Foreman and Whitehead all plead not guilty to being accessories to the murder of McVitie.

An eleventh man, Albert Donaghue, pleads guilty to the last charge. He was not in the dock yesterday.

Mr. Jones said that the link between the killing of McVitie and the shooting of George Cornell lay in Ronald Kray's remark to his twin, Reginald: "I have done my one. It is about time you did yours."

The Crown's case was that the gunman in the Blind Beggar public house who murdered Cornell was Ronald Kray and the brother to whom he went and from whom he received assistance was Reginald Kray.

In the second murder, the Crown said that McVitie was killed by Reginald Kray and the twin brother who urged him on was Ronald Kray.

Dealing with the shooting of George Cornell, Mr. Jones said that on the evening of his death in the Blind Beggar, Cornell was drinking with friends from about eight o'clock.

"It was the sort of scene one would encounter in any public house in the country.

"But then two men came into the saloon bar. They walked down the bar towards Cornell, who looked up and actually said: 'Look who's here.'

"One of these two men stood about five or six feet from Cornell and the other stood behind him. They both had guns in their hands. The one in front raised his arm, fired and shot Cornell through the forehead.

"Two other shots were fired, probably by the second man, but they did no harm. Cornell fell to the floor and the two men turned on their heel and walked out of the public house leaving him dying on the floor.

The two other shots, said Mr. Jones, were fired "to strike terror into anybody who was there in the public-house to make them keep their heads down."

He added: "It would make it much more difficult for those people to see and, subsequently, to be able to identify, either the man who fired the fatal shot or his companion.

"The case is that the leading man who fired the fatal shot was Ronald Kray and his companion was John Barrie."

'BARMAID SAW KRAY'

Mr. Jones said it was "a horrifying effrontery" when two men could walk into a public house and "in cold blood slay another human being."

He asked: "Who, within striking distance of such men, would be safe? Who would thereafter have the courage to come before the court and say who those men were?"

Mr. Jones continued: "I shall call before the court the barmaid. Some of us, fortunately, do not lack courage. She will tell you the man who fired the shot was Ronald Kray. She knew him."

Mr. Jones said Reginald Kray knew of the murder within a few minutes and immediately set about helping his brother Ronald.

MOVE TO NEW COURT

He went on: "There is a connection between these two murders and it is this: During that intervening period arguments took place from time to time between Ronald and Reginald Kray. They were not of any great importance — arguments do sometimes occur between relatives—but in the course of these arguments Ronald would say to his brother, 'I have done my one, it is about time you did yours.'

"That is a very real link which binds these murders together."

The trial continues today, but will be moved to the Old Bailey's Number One Court—slightly larger than the scene of yesterday's hearing.

The barmaid alleged by the prosecution to have seen Ronald Kray shoot down Cornell will give evidence today.

She will be taken to court under police guard. Metal screens have been erected inside the Old Bailey to shield her from view as she passes along the corridor to Number One Court.

JURY TOLD: DON'T EVEN ACCEPT A CUP OF TEA

THE all-male jury hearing the Kray case trial left the Old Bailey, and joined London's evening rush hour after the adjournment, followed by 24 Scotland Yard detectives.

The detectives — 23 men and one woman—had earlier slipped into court where each pair of detectives had been allocated a juror.

They were told the position he was sitting in the jury box.

The purpose of the brief visit to the court during the hearing was to see the face of the juryman each had been allotted.

The detectives have strict orders not to talk with the jurors they are guarding.

They followed the jurors home on bus, train, tube, car and foot. Some had to hitch lifts to keep up with the men they were shadowing.

The guards spent last night on watch in cars outside the jurors' homes.

They have been told not to accept any offers of hospitality—even a cup of tea.

The guards are working in shifts round the clock—and will trail the jurors back to the court again today.

Numbered men protest over 'cattle market'

THE Kray brothers won the first disputed point in their trial yesterday when they successfully protested against identifying placards being hung round their necks as they sat in the dock at the Old Bailey.

The decision to do without the placards followed an extraordinary scene in court during which nine of the ten men in the dock took their placards off. Several tore them up and Ronald Kray shouted out: "This is not a cattle market."

RONALD KRAY

The judge, Mr. Justice Melford Stevenson, had suggested that, because of the large number of men in the dock, placards would make identification easier.

LED AWAY

When it became obvious that only one of the defendants was prepared to accept this, the judge suggested that they should be taken back to the cells for the placards to be put on.

"It's not a question of imposing indignity on anybody," he said. "It's obviously extremely difficult in a crowded dock such as this for witnesses to refer to someone sitting in the third row. That is why it is going to be done."

It was as they were being led away that Ronald Kray and some of the other defendants ripped up their cardboard placards.

When they returned to the dock 35 minutes later, the placards had been removed.

Instead, numbers were pinned to the front of the wooden dock and plans of the seating arrangements for the three rows of defendants were distributed round the court.

REGINALD KRAY

Mr. John Platts-Mills, QC. for Ronald Kray, then rose to tell Mr. Justice Stevenson: "I have been asked by one of the accused to say how very much they appreciate the dispensation the court has allowed."

'RELIEF'

The judge replied: "That's a great relief."

In previous trials at the Old Bailey involving a number of defendants it has been the practice for them to wear numbered placards.

Until yesterday nobody is believed to have objected.

key before they could persuade any witness to talk about their murders, but how far they went or would have dared to go in the use of direct methods of intimidation on people above their own class or kind is questionable. Payne described Reggie as 'the bloody terror who would cut you for nothing and the endearingly awkward East End tough fused together', but Reggie never attempted to cut Payne, a superior type of criminal, though Payne eventually gave Reggie good cause to cut him for *something,* namely speaking a volume or two to the police. Significantly, too, Ronnie, who positively loved violence and hadn't hesitated to shoot Cornell in front of witnesses, never himself attacked Payne. At first, he sent the luckless McVitie to do the job for him; later, so Payne says, he imported a homosexual murderer named 'Junior' to kill both him and Superintendent Read, who headed the investigation that finally destroyed the Krays. Again, Pearson maintains that Ronnie's attitude to the police was one of both loathing and utter contempt, but one may suspect that here he was simply taking Ronnie's word for it. For Payne, by contrast, says that the police put Ronnie into a state of abject terror.

Again, it seems more than possible that Pearson's story of how Ronnie enjoyed humiliating an old peer of the realm, who was a consistent loser at Esmeralda's Barn, was invented by Ronnie himself. Pearson writes that after the peer had lost again, he'd ring up Ronnie at his East End home, and threaten suicide: 'All right, you silly old bastard,' Ronnie would say, 'don't waste gas by putting your head in the oven today. Come round to Vallance Road when I've had my shave and I'll see what I can do. Don't be late.' But Payne says that the Krays had an 'almost Victorian respect for titles'. If one accepts that, and one can hardly avoid doing so in view of their chronic pursuit of celebrities, it is impossible to believe that Ronnie would have dared speak to any peer as he told Pearson that he did, except in his wild imaginings.

However, Payne and Pearson are in broad, though not detailed, agreement about the Krays' association with organized crime in America. In fact, Payne claims to have come in contact with it himself, when he met with someone he calls 'K', an ex-robber, whom he describes as 'the right-hand man of the local syndicate'. The syndicate, he said, had £2,000,000 worth of stolen bearer bonds in Canada, but they were not negotiable there. Payne purchased £50,000 worth, at a quarter their face value, and brought them to Paris, where they were disposed of to the profit of the Krays as well as himself.

At the same time, it must be said that neither Payne nor Pearson appears to possess a deep knowledge of organized crime in America. For instance, Payne refers to 'Anastasios' when he means Anastasia, while Pearson tells how Ronnie met the 'top New York mafioso, Angelo Bruno' without realizing that even granted Bruno *is* the top mafioso, he does not come from New York at all but is boss in Philadelphia.

Apart from their traffic in stolen securities, no doubt the Krays did meet a number of American criminals, or former criminals, who were hopeful of getting a share of the profits from legalized gambling in London or anywhere else in Britain, and who may have supposed that the Krays could provide the necessary muscle. But the Krays were strictly cockneys, and though Ronnie evidently had dreams of building a national gangster empire, he had made little or no progress in doing so. It is difficult to believe, therefore, that a man of the stature of Angelo Bruno, who, if Gay Talese is right, was not only the boss in Philadelphia, but a member of the Mafia's nine-man national commission, could have taken the Krays' pretensions seriously.

At any rate, Pearson writes that when Ronnie went to New York in April 1968, 'Angelo Bruno had mysteriously left town' (or, in fact, had probably stayed at home), 'and so had the other leading *mafiosi* Ronnie had met and entertained in London'. Ronnie had to content himself with being entertained by Joe Kaufman, a little Jewish man who was later to be imprisoned in London for fraud. He was assured that Kaufman had 'powerful connections with the Mafia'. True, Payne tells a different story. He says that Ronnie did meet with Mafia chieftains in New York, whom he doesn't, however, identify. And when Ronnie was asked how he'd like to be entertained, he expressed his preference for a boy. 'It was a ticklish moment, because these good Catholics couldn't be relied on to be understanding about such tastes. But the boss slapped Ronnie on the shoulder saying "It takes a lot of balls that sort of thing", and got him a young man of his choosing'. But here Payne must have been relying on his imagination, for he had, at the time of Ronnie's visit to New York, ceased to have any contact with the Krays. They had been trying to have him killed.

His place in their criminal activities was in effect taken by an extraordinarily mysterious character named Alan Cooper. Cooper was a Jew, youngish and very rich; he was English-born, but had served in the American army, and travelled on an American passport. He owned a private bank in London, and in return for their protection agreed to help the Krays to dispose of stolen bonds. Cooper accompanied Ronnie to New York, and assured him that the fact that he was not only allowed into America but was treated by the immigration and customs officials with unusual deference was all due to the 'power of the Mafia'. Ronnie—and this shows how extremely simple-minded he must have been—believed him. For

Above: Ronnie and Reggie Kray with their mother and grandfather and (right) as professional boxers in 1952

The Regency Club where McVitie was heard to threaten to shoot the Kray twins, a threat which resulted in McVitie's execution

Below: Reggie Kray with Barbara Windsor

one thing that gangsters know to be incorruptible, and dare not tamper with, is federal agencies.

On his return Cooper told Ronnie that the reason why leading mafiosi had avoided him might have been because they'd heard the police were catching up with the Kray twins, and that a real show of strength was needed to restore the Mafia's faith in them. The answer would be a really spectacular murder; something reminiscent of the old Chicago days. And to carry this out, Cooper produced an oddly talented but fundamentally inefficient sort of potential killer named Elvey.

Cooper had previously used Elvey in an attempt to kill a man whom Ronnie, for no very good reason, wished to be killed. Elvey tried twice to bring this off, and by the most ingenious means; but on both occasions something went wrong at the last moment. This time the proposed victim was a Maltese nightclub owner named Caruana; and the plan was to blow him up with a charge of dynamite placed in his car. Elvey flew to Glasgow, where Cooper had a source, and picked up four sticks of dynamite. As he was about to board the return plane, the police arrested him. He was taken back to London under guard, interrogated by Superintendent Read, and made a full confession.

He named Cooper as his employer, and Read, who had no knowledge of Cooper at the time, was about to charge him with attempted murder, when Cooper told him the truth—or, at any rate, something that bore a resemblance to it. He admitted that he had been a crook when he helped the twins sell stolen bonds, but claimed that he was now a U.S. agent, controlled from Paris, and had been acting as a spy and agent provocateur. It had been essential to pretend to arrange the killings in order to assure the Krays of his loyalty; and equally essential that the person employed to carry them out should believe in them. But he had relied on Elvey's chronic inefficiency to guarantee his failure.

One may be certain at least that Ronald Kray would never have been granted a visa for his entry into the United States unless someone had had the power and authority to make special arrangements for it, and one may believe that that someone was, as Cooper said, his control officer in Paris. It is harder to see what the Americans hoped to gain out of having Ronnie in New York. Pearson quotes Cooper as saying 'We were counting on Ronnie meeting Meyer Lansky, the Las Vegas people, Angelo Bruno and the Gallo Brothers. But Ronnie was so hot that none of them would risk seeing him.' But

Ronnie was 'hot' in England, not in America. And if it really was fear of being seen with him in their own country that deterred them, why wasn't Cooper forewarned of this? After all, he had, according to his own account, flown several times to Washington to 'fix details' of the trip. Surely someone in the F.B.I. could have told him that the Mafia was scared, and that therefore it would be a waste of time, money and effort bringing Ronnie to New York. And what of little Kaufman, with his alleged Mafia connections? He had been trafficking in stolen American bonds at least since July 1966, when he was introduced by Charles Kray, the Kray twins' elder brother, to Alan Cooper at the Colony Club in London, and informed Cooper that he had $50,000 worth of stolen blue chip securities for sale. Pearson says that Kaufman did, in fact, make Ronnie's American trip thoroughly enjoyable for him by introducing him to 'half the deadbeat criminals' in New York. But shouldn't he also have known that he wouldn't be able to do any better?

One can, of course, perfectly understand—it has already been hinted at—why the leading racketeers in America should not wish to spend any time with a paranoid punk like Ronnie Kray. And even assuming some of them had imagined there was a real opportunity of getting in on gambling in Britain, and had come to England partly with the idea of enlisting the Krays' help, Cooper kept reminding Ronnie before he decided to authorize Caruana's murder that—to quote Pearson—'the question of which London gang was to look after the big gambling junkets from the States was still not decided'.

For all that, the reasons why the Americans should have thought it of such importance to allow Ronnie to visit New York remain a mystery. Maybe Cooper thought it would strengthen Ronnie's faith in him to be able to say it was all due to the Mafia. Maybe, because he was an obvious fantasist himself, he honestly believed that Bruno et al. would be falling over each other to get in touch with Ronnie. And maybe he persuaded his boss in Paris of this. Payne says, and Pearson broadly hints, that Cooper was working specifically for the United States Treasury Bureau of Narcotics. If this was so, and the Krays were suspected of involvement in narcotics smuggling, the facilitation of Ronnie's entry into America would be more understandable. For the Bureau has been obsessed with the idea that the Mafia is a 'secret international organization'. At a time when the Kefauver Committee clearly considered Frank Costello the number one enemy, the Bureau said that Costello (and others) took their orders from Lucky Luciano, who was the real boss both before and after his deportation to Italy. Further, the Bureau alleged, apparently without proof, that before his death in 1962 Luciano was responsible for the smuggling of dope into the United States. And shortly after Burton B. Turkus claimed in 1950 that the Mafia had been virtually extinct for the past twenty years, the Bureau announced, through John T. Cusack, its district supervisor, that it had amassed conclusive evidence of the Mafia's threatening existence over the past thirty years!

However, there is no reason to believe that the Kray twins were involved in the narcotics business, though doubtless they would have liked to be. They would have liked to be in any business that could have fulfilled Ronnie's fantasy of him and Reggie becoming the big American gangsters. But unfortunately for the two of them they weren't in America; and if they had been one cannot imagine them advancing much beyond the role of muscle men; men without much brain or organizing ability, but with a readiness to kill and a continual inclination to violence.

The strangest thing about them is the story of their relationship with Frank Mitchell. Ronnie had first met Mitchell when they were locked up together at Wandsworth Prison in 1956, and he became his friend. Mitchell was a hugely built and enormously strong mental defective. He had escaped from a mental hospital where, if anywhere, he belonged, and threatened an elderly couple with an axe, which won him the press-inspired appellation of the 'Mad Axeman'. The madman was thereupon jailed, with an illogicality that the press apparently did not notice. In due course, he was birched for attacking a prison officer; previously he had been given sixteen strokes of the cat-o'-nine-tails. These punishments, incidentally, are no longer permitted—even for prisoners who have never been certified!

Ronnie Kray (after a couple of spells at the Spring Grove Hospital for the Insane, and an escape) was released from Wandsworth in 1959. But the following year Reggie was sent there for a while, and he also liked Mitchell. The twins kept in touch with him during the years that followed. They arranged for his defence on a charge of attempted murder, of which he was acquitted. Reggie gave him a radio, and they were in continuous communication. Meanwhile Mitchell was transferred to Dartmoor, where it was at last realized that brutality was a useless way of dealing with this poor, potentially violent

Above: A typical cell in Dartmoor

defective of herculean strength. Instead, the governor tried kindness, and the officers recognized soon enough that this was what had been needed all along. Mitchell became an unusually trusted prisoner, and was relying on the governor to work for and eventually win a release for him.

But he had no true stability. In August 1966, five months after the murder of Cornell, the twins suddenly announced their intention of 'springing' him so that he could be home for Christmas. He was overjoyed, and supposed that to escape was what he had always been yearning to do.

The affinity the Krays felt for Mitchell may have been essentially protective. Here was a man more simple-minded than they were, more obviously barmy, but with just as great a propensity for violence. They could at one and the same time admire him and be convinced of their own superiority to him. But the reason why they suddenly decided to spring him is unexplained. The theory suggested by the prosecution when the Krays were tried for Mitchell's murder was that they wanted him as a strong-arm man: an explanation which Pearson rightly regards as absurd. But Pearson's own theory, which he calls the 'truth', that the idea of freedom for Mitchell was a 'simple exercise in underworld public relations' seems hardly less grotesque. One cannot imagine any of the American racketeers being the slightest bit impressed; and even Charles Kray told Reggie he was mad to think of it. For aiding and abetting an escape is a serious offence, and one which in Mitchell's case they could never have hoped to conceal, if he had been allowed to show his face in public again. But they realized that too late.

Below: Frank Mitchell's hideout in East London

It was an easy matter to arrange Mitchell's escape, for he was allowed virtual freedom on the moors during working hours. He was driven to London and lodged in a ground-floor flat in the East End. Members of the Firm took it in turn to guard him, and Reggie called on him regularly, though Ronnie, who was suffering from a kind of breakdown, stayed away. He was helped to write a letter to the press, explaining that the reason he had left Dartmoor was to draw attention to his plight and ask for a possible release date. As the days passed, Mitchell grew increasingly restless; his guards did their best to humour him, but warned Reggie that unless he introduced a woman into the household there would be serious trouble. Reggie produced a nightclub hostess named Lisa, whom he paid well for her services. She went to bed with

Charles Kray (third from left) and Reggie Kray (far right) on their way to prison, 1969

Mitchell and stayed there for two days. Later, she described him as the most virile man she had ever known.

But this was only a respite. Mitchell commanded one of his guards to give him his gun, and the terrified man obeyed. He wept and raged. Finally, he issued Reggie with an ultimatum: if the twins could not find him a better place to live, he would get in touch with his parents. He had a gun now, and would use it on anyone who tried to stop him. Reggie seemingly capitulated. Mitchell would be going, within forty-eight hours, to Ronnie's place in Kent, where he could lead a life of leisure, with servants, and all the animals he wanted, and, most importantly of all, with Lisa, with whom he had fallen in love. 'The only girl I've ever loved', he wrote on a Christmas card.

He left on Christmas Eve, though without Lisa. She had confided to a guard that though she had told him she was going, she hadn't any serious intention of doing so. When it came to the point, the excuse was made that

it would be too risky taking them together. She'd be following separately, and would probably be there as soon as he was. He accepted this quite happily. He gave her a kiss, and went off with a man called Albert Donaghue, who had come to drive him to Kent. And he was never seen again, either alive or dead.

Albert Donaghue, however, was seen as a witness for the prosecution at the trial of the Kray twins and Frederick Foreman for Mitchell's murder. His evidence—the evidence of a man himself involved in the crime charged—could not be accepted without corroboration, and since the jury found no sufficient corroboration of it, all three defendants were acquitted.

The story of their concern with Frank Mitchell typifies the whole of their criminal career. They acted on impulse; and in Ronnie's case at least it was the impulse of a madman. They were dangerous criminals certainly, but not notably successful ones. Certainly not equipped to bring organized crime to Britain.

PART 2 POLITICAL CRIME

1/Sacco and Vanzetti

On the night of 10 August 1927, twelve days before the execution of Sacco and Vanzetti, A. J. Cook, the British miners' leader, addressed a London crowd estimated at thirty thousand strong: 'I warn you and I warn America that if they murder these two men we will get even with them. I ask you to take off your hats and pledge yourselves to get even. If America kills these two men, it will be murder and we will repay.'[19]

Opposite: Sacco (right) and Vanzetti Inset: *Daily News*, 24 August 1927

That, of course, was an idle claim, and made, incidentally, against the wrong party, for it wasn't the United States of America but the Commonwealth of Massachusetts which had convicted the two men and sentenced them to death. Nonetheless it is an indication of the strength of feeling that had been whipped up, not only in Britain, but throughout the civilized world, about a case which, seven years before, a reporter from a New York socialist newspaper had decided was 'nothing—just a couple of wops in a jam'.[20]

In June 1927 H. G. Wells wrote that if Sacco and Vanzetti were executed it would be the blackest crime in history. Wells believed without question (having read Professor Felix Frankfurter on the subject) what others among Europe's most illustrious citizens, such as John Galsworthy, Thomas Mann, Fritz Kreisler and Albert Einstein, also believed: namely, that Sacco and Vanzetti had been convicted of murder, not because they were guilty of this or any other crime, but because they were anarchists. But today, nearly fifty years later, it is no longer possible to accept this conclusion so unquestioningly.

It is true that in 1920, when Sacco and Vanzetti were arrested, America was in the grip of a mammoth anti-red scare; and thousands of foreigners suspected of so-called radicalism were being illegally rounded up and deported. On 24 December the previous year an unsuccessful hold-up attempt had taken place in Bridgewater, Massachusetts. Then on 15 April 1920 a daylight robbery was perpetrated in the main street of South Braintree. A paymaster and his guard Berardelli were carrying the payroll of the Slater and Morrell Shoe Company when two bandits opened fire and deliberately gunned them to death. The murderers seized the loot and made their getaway in a stolen Buick, which was occupied by at least one other man besides the driver.

Two days later the car was found abandoned in the Manley Woods, a few miles outside the town, and there were tracks of a smaller car leading away from the spot. When Chief Stewart of the Bridgewater Police viewed the scene, he exclaimed involuntarily, 'the men who did this job knew no God.' He learned from eye-witnesses that this hold-up as well as the previous one at Bridgewater had been committed by men who looked like foreigners, and he jumped to the conclusion that both crimes must have been the work of the same godless band of red robbers.

Then Stewart happened on a definite lead. He discovered that a known Italian anarchist named Coacci—Stewart had secured a deportation order against him—was sharing a shack in West Bridgewater with another Italian, a certain Mike Boda. Police enquiries revealed that this Boda had been observed driving a Buick a few days before the South Braintree hold-up, and that he was the owner of a smaller car, an Overland, which had been towed to a garage for repairs some time after the crime. Stewart arranged for the proprietor of the garage, a Mr Simon Johnson, to inform the police as soon as Boda came to pick up his Overland car.

This didn't happen until late in the evening of 5 May, and by then Coacci had already been deported. But Boda was not alone. With him were a man called Orceani, who was standing beside his motorcycle, and also Nicola Sacco and Bartolemo Vanzetti.

At this time, Sacco was 29 and Vanzetti was 32. Both came from comparatively affluent peasant homes in Italy; both had been Republicans who emigrated to America before the First World War in search of freedom and plenty and had met with disillusionment. Vanzetti, who was much the better read and more gifted of the two, was to write in Italian during the long years of imprisonment that preceded his execution, 'how well I remember standing at the Battery, upon my arrival in New York, alone with a few poor belongings in the way of clothes, and very little money. Until yesterday, I was among folks who understood me. This morning I seemed to have awakened in a world where my language meant little more to the natives than the pitiful noises of a dumb animal. Where was I to go? What was I to do? Here was the Promised Land. The elevated rattled by and did not answer. The automobiles and trolleys sped by heedless of me.'[21]

Though they arrived in America at the same time, they did not meet and become friends until several years later. They were by then fervent anarchists, and in 1917 they fled to Mexico to avoid the draft. Neither of them had a criminal record, but both believed that violence was permissible under certain circumstances. Sacco was now working in a shoe factory at Stoughton, and lived in a house on his employer's land. He was a devoted family man, with an attractive, titian-haired wife, Rosina, a son, Dante, aged six, and a daughter on the way, who was to be named Ines. Vanzetti was a bachelor. He earned his living peddling fish in Plymouth.

While Simon Johnson talked to Boda, Mrs Johnson went to telephone the police. When she got back, Boda and Orceani had already driven off on the motorcycle, having decided not to take the car, and she saw Sacco and Vanzetti leave on foot. Shortly afterwards they boarded a trolley car for Brockton, but they did not reach their destination. On the way there they were arrested and taken to Brockton police station where Chief Stewart was awaiting them. They were both found to be armed: Sacco with a .32 pistol and twenty-two cartridges of various makes; Vanzetti with a fully loaded revolver and four shotgun shells, one of them a Winchester. The discovery served as the immediate pretext for holding them, for neither man possessed a licence to carry fire-arms.

They were examined separately by Stewart, and both gave him mendacious answers. For instance, they denied any knowledge of Boda, and claimed they had gone to West Bridgewater to see a man called Pappi. Next morning, the district attorney, Frederick G. Katzmann, took over the examination. He did not actually tell them what crimes they were suspected of committing, but he gave some very broad hints; and again they lied to him. It was these lies that were ultimately to destroy them.

Ironically, however, Chief Stewart's (and Katzmann's) theory of a red robber gang was unsupportable by any evidence. Efforts to trace the South Braintree loot proved abortive. The police failed to tie Boda and Orceani to either of the two hold-ups. And they were unable to tie even Sacco to the Bridgewater affair, because the factory clock left no doubt that he had been at work all day on 24 December 1919. Nevertheless, they had a strong enough case to convict Vanzetti on the Bridgewater charge and did so without any reference to the fact that he was an anarchist. There were eye-witnesses to identify him as the bandit who had fired at the moving truck with a shotgun; there was an empty Winchester shell which had been picked up at the scene of the crime and was similar to the one found in Vanzetti's possession on his arrest. Vanzetti's only defence was an alibi furnished by thirteen of his Italian friends and neighbours in Plymouth, who testified that he had been busy selling eels on the morning when the hold-up took place. But they were, all of them, pretty wobbly under cross-examination. And Vanzetti virtually convicted himself in the end through his failure to take the witness stand. Whether this was his own decision or not is one of many aspects of the whole case that will presumably always be in dispute. Probably his counsel thought it highly inadvisable to expose a radical and a draft-dodger to cross-examination, but left the final choice to him.

At the Bridgewater trial of Vanzetti, Judge Webster Thayer, the arch-villain of the story for all those who thought Sacco and Vanzetti were murdered, made his first appearance. He was a man of nearly 63, who looked ten years older and had a voice, so one of his enemies said, 'like a thin strip of steel'. But now his charge to the jury seemed eminently fair: 'The defendant says he could not have committed the alleged crimes because he was in Plymouth. If you find such to be a fact, that is the end of the case. Now you must stand between the parties with fairness, with impartiality. Because the witnesses are Italians no inference should be drawn against them. People are supposed to be honest, to be truthful, to be innocent. You have seen them, you have heard them, you have looked into their faces . . .'[22]

Still, Thayer probably ought to have disqualified himself from presiding at the joint trial of Sacco and Vanzetti for murder. Instead, he asked for the job; and even though he may have succeeded in giving an impression of fairness in his conduct of the trial, he undoubtedly was intensely prejudiced against the defendants. In private, he called them 'those anarchist bastards'.[23]

The murder trial opened nearly a year after Vanzetti had been convicted of the attempted hold-up at Bridgewater, and was held in Dedham, a residential suburb of Boston. The case for the prosecution was opened by Herbert Williams, the assistant district attorney. He promised eye-witness evidence to prove that Vanzetti had travelled by train from Plymouth to Braintree on the morning of 15 April; evidence that would identify him as the driver of the getaway car; and evidence to identify Sacco as one of the bandits who had done the actual shooting. The assistant district attorney also promised to show that a cap that had been found near the scene of the murder belonged to Sacco; that the bullet that actually caused Berardelli's death was fired from his gun; and that the revolver found in Vanzetti's possession on his arrest had belonged to Berardelli.

Now all this evidence might, if left on its own, have

been rejected. The identification testimony was especially weak, since it was refuted by a larger number of witnesses called on behalf of the defence. But the trouble was the lies that both of them had told Stewart and Katzmann at the time of their arrest. This indicated 'consciousness of guilt', and their leading lawyer decided that the only way to overcome it was to reveal their whole life story, which would show why, as anarchists, they had been afraid, first of betraying their political associates and secondly of putting themselves in danger of deportation. Thayer could claim afterwards that this was a course taken against his advice, and it certainly gave Katzmann, the district attorney, virtually unlimited opportunities to cross-examine them on matters that otherwise Thayer could not have allowed. Much of Katzmann's cross-examination was purely inflammatory, but not all of it. If he deliberately encouraged the jury to condemn these two men as draft-dodgers, he was also able to arouse doubts about whether the lies they had told him at the Brockton police station had really been for the purposes which they now claimed. For example, he asked Vanzetti whether he had intended to address a meeting of returned soldiers at Brockton on 10 May (1920), and Vanzetti could not deny it, even if he'd wished to, because the draft of a circular announcing the meeting had been found in Sacco's pocket. It contained the words: 'You have fought in the wars, and have worked for capitalists and tried their ways.' If Vanzetti had really been so alarmed about the threat of deportation when he was arrested on 5 May, why should he have been prepared to talk revolution at a public meeting five days later?

The same point was made against Sacco. He admitted that he had meant to attend the meeting himself, and that he was going to pass out some five hundred circulars to his 'radical friends', inviting them to come as well. 'And you still say the real reason why you told me so many falsehoods', said Katzmann, 'was because you were afraid of your Radical friends being turned up?'

'Sure,' said Sacco.

'Are those answers consistent? Do you understand what consistent means?'

'Consistent to me.'[24]

The trial lasted nearly seven weeks, and on the morning of 14 July, when Judge Thayer was due to deliver his charge, the bench was banked with flowers. 'Mr Foreman', he began, 'and gentlemen of the jury, the Commonwealth of Massachusetts called upon you to render a most important service. Although you knew such a service would be arduous and tiresome, yet you, like the true soldier, responded to that call in the spirit of supreme American loyalty. There is no better word in the English language than loyalty.'[25]

It was hardly the sort of introduction to counteract any prejudice the jury might be feeling towards these two reds and draft-dodgers. However, Thayer reviewed the evidence with apparent impartiality, though he placed very much more emphasis on the issue of consciousness of guilt than he did on any of the other evidence for or against the defendants; and it was in fact this issue which he considered resolved by the verdict, and which he would rely on for his rejection of all the motions for a new trial in the years ahead. The jury returned after an absence of some seven hours with their verdict of guilty.

'What am I going to do?' Mrs Sacco screamed. 'I've got two children. Oh, Nick! They kill my man! They kill my man!'[26]

Mrs Sacco imagined her man was going to be led straight to the execution chamber; and in England this would have been nearly true, in comparison with what actually happened. In fact, under Massachusetts law, the defendants could not even be sentenced until all the legal resources which were open to them, and which they chose to use, had been exhausted. They had a Defence Committee behind them; and they had a leading counsel, for whom the fight had only just begun. His name was Fred H. Moore; he was a radical himself, and a professional defender of labour leaders who ran foul of the law. 'That long haired anarchist from California', Judge Thayer called him behind his back; and Moore, who was not a member of the Massachusetts bar, could hardly have been more antipathetic to Thayer. He was as free with money as he was with women.

But he turned the Sacco and Vanzetti case into a minor national cause, and he laid the foundations for its becoming a major international cause. For four years he fought, using propaganda to arouse sympathy for his clients, sympathy to obtain funds, funds to employ inquiry agents, inquiry agents to unearth new evidence. Moore filed seven motions in all, and it was not until 1 October 1924 that Thayer finally disposed of them.

For Moore himself that was the end. He had been having growing disagreements with the Defence Committee. Moreover, Sacco, who believed, probably wrongly, that Moore had been exploiting his case, wrote calling himself Moore's 'implacable enemy'. Moore very reluctantly resigned from the case, after it had been his whole

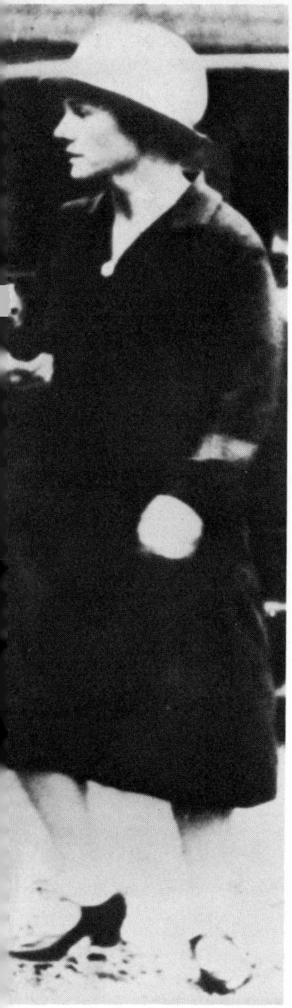

Above: Mrs Sacco (right) on her way to visit her husband in prison

Left: Judge Webster Thayer who presided over Sacco and Vanzetti's trial

life for the past four years, and returned, penniless, to California.

His place was taken by William G. Thompson, a deeply conservative Boston lawyer, but with a burning faith in the innocence of Sacco and Vanzetti. In May 1926 he filed a further motion for a new trial. It was based partly on a confession by a convicted murderer, named Medeiros, that he had taken part in the Braintree hold-up, which was the work of a professional gang of Italian criminals; and partly on an allegation, sworn to by two former agents of the U.S. Department of Justice, that the Department had agreed to help the district attorney get a conviction in return for his assistance in securing information that would render Sacco and Vanzetti liable to deportation if he failed.

'Every Federal agent who knew anything about it', Thompson said in asking Thayer to grant his motion, 'believed these men to be innocent of murder. Every one of them believed they ought to be deported. They were anarchists, they did not believe in organized government or private property. Oh, how those words will ring around this world. The man who does not believe in private property in America may be killed, whether he is guilty or not. Now, I say to your Honor I do not care whether you believe Medeiros or do not believe Medeiros. I do not care if these men—Sacco and Vanzetti—are guilty of murder, this state cannot afford to execute men after a trial conducted in that way.'[27]

On 23 October Thayer denied the motion in a 25,000-word judgement that included these contemptuous words: 'Since the trial before the Jury of these cases, a new type of disease would seem to have developed. It might be called "lego-psychic neurosis" or "hysteria" which means; "a belief in the existence of something which in fact and truth has no such existence".'[28]

This shocked even the staid *Boston Herald,* which announced its conviction that Thayer was incapable of acting as an impartial arbitrator. Not long afterwards, Professor Felix Frankfurter of the Harvard Law School published his famous denunciation of Thayer's decision: 'It cannot be described otherwise than as a farrago of misquotations, misrepresentations, suppressions and mutilations. The opinion is literally honeycombed with demonstrable errors, and confused with a spirit alien to judicial utterance.'[29]

It was Felix Frankfurter's attack that sent the world outcry into high gear. But one may doubt if much notice would have been taken of it, at any rate outside America, if

MADEIROS, SACCO, VANZETTI DIED IN CHAIR THIS MORNING

Electrocuted in That Order Soon After Midnight—All Reject Religious Consolation to the Last—Two Make Statements

POLICE TAKE 156 OF "DEATH WATCH"

Sacco and Vanzetti Demonstration in Front Of State House Is Broken Up Several Times—Some Rearrested

With the taking into custody of 23 adults and three juveniles shortly after 5 o'clock police brought the total number of arrests of State House pickets yesterday to 156, there having been 130 persons arrested previously

the pickets and the activity of the police.

All the prisoners were bailed out at police stations and released by Commissioners Joseph Fahey and William Brophy, with the exception of Helen Crowe, who refused bail but later accepted it when she was taken to the City Prison.

PRISON IS GUARDED BY VERITABLE ARMY

Six Establishments of Police on Duty

Riot Squads and Machine-Gun Groups at Stragetic Points

Mobilized silently and quickly, with the precision of a well-trained army, police of six different establishments representing the Boston and Cambridge departments, the Metropolitan District Commission, State Police Patrol, Boston & Maine Railroad detectives and the prison force united last night to guard the State Prison at Charlestown and its vicinity during the straining hours preceding and following the execution of Sacco, Vanzetti and Madei-

CELESTINO MADEIROS

NICOLA SACCO

BARTOLOMEO VANZETTI

LAST-MINUTE PLEAS

MEN REITERATED THEIR INNOCENCE

Madeiros in Stupor—Other Two Face Death Calmly

Judges Holmes, Anderson And Lowell Refuse Final Appeals

Boston Daily Globe,
23 August 1927

the Communists hadn't suddenly awoken to the propaganda potential of the case back in June 1925, and adopted, or tried to adopt, Sacco and Vanzetti as their own. They didn't get any distance with the Defence Committee in Boston, but through a front organization they were wholly responsible for making the case the giant issue it became in Europe. Wells, Galsworthy, Kreisler and all were in a sense their victims. Even Mussolini felt obliged to tell his people, 'I have done everything compatible with international law to save Sacco and Vanzetti from execution.'[30] The motives of the Communists were, of course, cynical in the extreme. They neither knew nor cared whether Sacco and Vanzetti were guilty or innocent of murder; and certainly these two anarchists would have been shot or imprisoned as political offenders in the Soviet Union. But as sworn enemies of capitalism, who were sooner or later to be unjustly executed, Sacco and Vanzetti were invaluable.

One American liberal at least remained aloof from the hubbub. Oliver Wendell Holmes, Justice of the U.S. Supreme Court, wrote to Harold Laski* in London: 'I doubt if anyone would say there was no evidence warranting a conviction. I cannot but ask myself why there is so much greater interest in red than black. A thousand-fold worse cases of negroes come up from time to time, but the world does not worry about them . . . and I think your public and literary men had better have kept their gentle mouths shut. My prejudices are all with Felix's book, but they are still stronger against the run of shriekers—the lovers of justice who have emphasised their love by blowing up a building or two . . .'[31]

* But Laski's attack on capital punishment shows that in 1939 he was still convinced of Sacco's and Vanzetti's innocence.

An appeal against Thayer's denial of Thompson's motion was rejected by the Supreme Court of the Commonwealth of Massachusetts on 5 April 1927. And four days later, after listening impassively to a fairly short tirade from Sacco and a much longer one from Vanzetti, Thayer spoke the words he had waited nearly six years to speak. He pronounced sentence of death.

The one recourse left was a petition for clemency to the Governor of Massachusetts, Alvin T. Fuller, a conservative and self-made millionaire. Fuller appointed a committee of three to advise him: Abott Lawrence Lowell, president of Harvard University, Samuel W. Stratton, president of the Massachusetts Institute of Technology, and Robert Grant, a retired probate judge. They were a distinguished, and one would have thought a fundamentally impartial, group of men, but after extensive hearings they found no compelling reason to advise a commutation of sentence, nor any reason for believing that Thayer had prejudiced the jury, though they thought him guilty of a grave breach of decorum in his conversations off the bench both during and after the trial.

And so, as the *Boston Herald* put it, 'the time for all discussion was over', though it wasn't, of course. For years after they were dead, the Sacco and Vanzetti case remained the inspiration of poems, novels, plays. In that sense, excepting only the crucifixion, there has probably never been a case to equal it. In the last twenty years alone, there have been no fewer than four books published about it; and there are probably more to come.

One thing above all is remembered by those who are still convinced of their innocence; the words that Vanzetti is supposed to have uttered: 'If it had not been for these thing, I might have lived out my life talking at street corners to scorning men. I might have die, unmarked, unknown, a failure. Now we are not a failure. This is our career and our triumph. Never in our full life could we hope to do such work for tolerance, for joostice, for man's onderstanding of man as now we do by accident. Our words—our lives—our pains—nothing! The taking of our lives—lives of good shoe-maker and poor fish-peddler—all! That last moment belongs to us—that agony is our triumph.'

It is almost certainly a myth that Vanzetti ever spoke those actual words, for they have a form and coherence which he certainly lacked—at least when speaking English. They were attributed to him by a reporter who was allowed to interview both the condemned men; and the reporter was Phil Strong, later to become a successful novelist. Strong attributed words to Sacco, who spoke worse English than Vanzetti, which in their way were just as moving, though they were never to have any place in the legend: 'First they give me basket to weave like children. Then I sit alone—seven years—thousands of days—and all for say man's nature can be perfect—day after day—nothing do, breathe, eat, sit up, lie down—because I think man innerly noble—not beast.'[32]

But it is not myth that the good shoe-maker and the poor fish-pedlar were, ultimately, their own best advocates. Vanzetti was self-educated and Sacco was hardly educated at all, but they were able to inspire a passionate belief in their innocence in many who had no sympathy with their politics. They could even make some of their foes conscious of their human tragedy. Herbert Williams, the assistant district attorney, broke down and wept when they were convicted.

Nor is it myth that Sacco wrote in a farewell letter to his son: 'Dante, I say once more to love and be nearest to your mother and the beloved ones in these sad days, and I am sure that with your brave heart and kind goodness they feel less discomfort. And you will not forget to love me a little for I do—O, Sonny! thinking so much and so often of you.'[33]

It is hard to believe that the man who wrote that letter could have committed the ruthless crime he was convicted of. It is even harder to believe that Vanzetti died with a lie on his lips. 'I wish to tell you', he said, 'that I am innocent and that I have never committed any crime but sometimes some sin. I wish to forgive some people for what they are now doing to me.'[34]

Yet though large holes were torn in the case against Sacco and Vanzetti, and larger holes have been torn in it since, the crucial part of it—their alleged 'consciousness of guilt'—has never been convincingly destroyed. One feels certain that the view of Sacco and Vanzetti as two martyrs, 'murdered' by the Commonwealth of Massachusetts because they were anarchists, though it may still be good Communist theory, is bad history. But one may feel equally certain that they were not ordinary criminals. The loot was never found on them. It was never seen again. And they may have been unjustly, though not *unreasonably,* convicted. Indeed, it seems certain that they must have been innocent, unless they believed that robbery and murder were justified in the service of their cause. In other words, their anarchism can have been the only reason for their guilt.

Were they guilty, therefore? One's instinct is to say no. But one cannot answer without a true understanding of the depth and quality of their faith, and that one cannot have unless one shares or has once shared it. Vanzetti wrote a letter near the end: 'Oh, friend, the anarchism is as beauty as a woman for me, perhaps even more since it include all the rest and me and her. Calm, serene, honest, natural, viril [*sic*], muddy and celestial at once, austere, heroic, fearless, *fatal,* generous, and *implacable*—all these and more it is' (my italics). And the last words that Sacco ever spoke were '*Viva l'Anarchia*'.[35]

Perhaps they sought a posthumous revolution through their martyrdom. Or perhaps they really believed, as they professed to believe, that only an immediate revolution could save them from the electric chair. But it remains at least a possibility that they risked what happened to them in the end by committing acts of violence for the anarchism they loved.

Sacco and Vanzetti's hearse on its way into the mortuary

JULIUS ROSENBERG and his wife Ethel, who have been sentenced to death by an American Federal Court, photographed yesterday in New York. They were convicted last week of obtaining atomic secrets and passing them to Russia.

In 1953 America was again caught up in a red scare. And the execution of the Rosenbergs was in some ways comparable with that of Sacco and Vanzetti. Throughout the world it provoked protests, not quite so loud, but still uproarious, which though they came from many sincere humanitarians—the Pope felt obliged to draw President Eisenhower's attention to the appeals for clemency he had received—were none the less Communist-inspired.

The story begins with the arrest in February 1950 of Dr Klaus Fuchs, the German-born nuclear physicist, who confessed to the British authorities that he had transmitted secret atomic intelligence to Russian agents. Dr Fuchs was sentenced to fourteen years' imprisonment, and having served his sentence (less time off for good behaviour) was flown by a seemingly obliging British government back to East Germany. However, near the beginning of his time in a British prison, he had been interviewed by F.B.I. agents and supplied them with information that led to the arrest in America of Harry Gold. Gold confessed willingly, even eagerly, stating inter alia that while Dr Fuchs was working on the atom bomb project in America he had served as a courier between Dr Fuchs and Yakovlev, a Russian vice-consul in New York. Further, he supplied information that made possible the arrest of other American nationals who had been engaged during the concluding months of the war in a conspiracy to commit espionage on behalf of the Soviet Union.

Gold was tried on 9 December 1950 and sentenced to thirty years. On 15 June 1950, as a result of his confession, David Greenglass had been arrested.

Back in 1944 and 1945 Greenglass, an enlisted man, was employed as a machinist in the Los Alamos laboratories of the Manhattan (atom bomb) Project. In June 1945 he was living with his wife Ruth in a one-room apartment in Albuquerque (New Mexico), which is near Los Alamos, and there he was visited early in the morning of Sunday, 3 June, by Harry Gold. Gold, according to his own story, had been instructed by his master Yakovlev to stop off at Albuquerque on his way back to New York from an important clandestine meeting in Santa Fe with Dr Fuchs. Before departing on his mission, he had received from Yakovlev a piece of onionskin paper on which was written the address of Greenglass and the recognition signal he was to use, 'I come from Julius'. This information he had memorized and had then destroyed the piece of paper. Yakovlev had also given him half of one side of a Jell-o box, jaggedly torn, which was to serve as a further means of identification; the Greenglasses, Yakovlev said, would be in possession of the other matching half. Gold had been assured by Yakovlev that David Greenglass would have some important information for him, and he had understood that Ruth Greenglass was a party to her husband's espionage.

David opened the door when Gold arrived at the Greenglasses' apartment. Gold said, 'I come from Julius', and then produced his half of the Jell-o box side. Ruth Greenglass was present, and apparently had the matching half of the Jell-o box side in her handbag. David explained that since Gold's visit was unexpected, he hadn't any material ready and would need time to prepare it. Gold said he would return for the material in the afternoon. As he was about to take his leave, Ruth Greenglass remarked that she had spoken with Julius before she left New York (late in February) to come to Albuquerque. Though Gold had no idea who the Julius in the recognition signal might be, the Greenglasses assumed it was David's brother-in-law Julius Rosenberg.

David prepared his material. It included some sketches of a lens mould, upon which he had been working at Los Alamos, a description of how this was set up as an experiment, a description of the experiment itself, a list of possible espionage recruits at Los Alamos, and some information about the test explosion of the atom bomb

that was scheduled to take place about a month later at Alamogordo, New Mexico. He put this material in an envelope, and Gold duly picked it up. David received an envelope in return from Gold; it contained $500. Before they parted, David told Gold that he expected to be in New York on furlough around Christmas, and that if Gold should wish to get in touch with him, he could always do so by calling his brother-in-law Julius Rosenberg. He gave Gold Julius's telephone number.

The F.B.I. arrested David Greenglass on 15 June 1950. He was no less willing to confess than Gold had been, and was more generously treated. He was sentenced to only fifteen years. Ruth Greenglass, who also admitted to a part in the conspiracy, was not prosecuted at all.

According to their testimony, it was the Rosenbergs who had tempted them to commit espionage, though not with the lure of gain, or at any rate not with the lure of any substantial gain. Julius had told Ruth, who was living in New York at the time, but was planning to visit Albuquerque shortly, that 'friends' (who he implied were Russian agents) had told him that David was working on the atom bomb, and that he believed the secrets of the atom bomb should be shared by the United States with its ally, the Soviet Union. For that reason he wanted information from David which he could pass on to the Russians. Ruth at first demurred, but was eventually persuaded by Ethel Rosenberg (David's sister) that it was her duty to give David Julius's message, and she did so. David, like Ruth before him, showed some initial reluctance to do as Julius wished, but after sleeping on it he decided to accept the proposition. When Ruth returned to New York in the first week of December 1944, she brought Julius information that included a description of the Los Alamos project and the real names of four famous scientists who were working there under cover.

Left: Dr Klaus Fuchs (standing left) with members of staff at the Atomic Energy Research Establishment and (above) on his way back to East Germany after his release from prison

In January 1945 David himself came to New York on a three-week furlough; he supplied Julius with some sketches of a high-explosive lens mould used in atomic experiments and some accompanying descriptive material. The sketches were less detailed than the ones David was subsequently to prepare for Harry Gold. The descriptive material was typed by Ethel from David's manuscript.

Julius had decided that Ruth should leave New York and set up house in Albuquerque, so that she might be able to pass David's material to an intermediary. One night, when the Greenglasses were dining at the Rosenbergs' apartment, Julius and Ethel took Ruth into the kitchen. There Julius tore the side of a Jell-o box in half, and told Ruth that the intermediary, whoever it might be, would be carrying the other half. When Ruth returned to the living room, she told David of this arrangement. 'That's very clever', David exclaimed. 'The simplest things', said Julius, 'are always clever.'[36]

A further act in the conspiracy took place before David returned to his work at Los Alamos. He borrowed his father's car and drove one night, at Julius's request, to a prearranged outdoor meeting place—somewhere on First Avenue between 42nd and 59th Street. As soon as Julius saw him, he went away and came back with an unidentified Russian, who got into the car and told David to drive around the area. While David did so, his Russian companion plied him with questions about the lens mould, the majority of which David was unable to answer. He brought the car to a stop at the original meeting place, where Julius was still standing. The Russian got out, and rejoined Julius. David drove home.

Ruth Greenglass left New York to set up house in Albuquerque at the end of February. She had then been told by Julius that an intermediary would meet her outside a Safeway store (which he named) in the afternoon of either the last Saturday in April or the first Saturday in May. In mid-April, however, Ruth had a miscarriage, and she wrote about this to Ethel who replied that 'a member of the family' would meet her on either the last Saturday in May or the Saturday before that. Ruth, accordingly, spent the afternoons of both days waiting in front of the Safeway store; on the second occasion David stood vigil with her. But no intermediary turned up. No intermediary appeared until the morning of 3 June, when he came unheralded in the person of Harry Gold.

In September, David had another furlough, and he and Ruth spent it in New York. David told Julius that, as a result of overhearing conversations and making discreet inquiries, he thought he had a 'pretty good description of the atom bomb'. Julius asked him to prepare his material at once, and paid him $200 as an advance. David produced, inter alia, a cross-section of the atom bomb, together with twelve pages of explanation. The Greenglasses (Ruth had made some effort to dissuade David from preparing the material) went to the Rosenbergs' apartment to deliver it. Ruth and Ethel corrected the grammar of the explanatory pages, and once again Ethel typed them.

That, briefly, was the story told by the Greenglasses. Largely on the basis of it, Julius Rosenberg was arrested on 16 June 1950 and Ethel Rosenberg on 11 August. On

Julius and Ethel Rosenberg being escorted into the Federal Court in New York, 1950

5 April 1951, after a three-week trial, they were sentenced to death by Judge Irving R. Kaufman, who, unprecedentedly, neither sought nor received a recommendation from the jury. On 19 June 1954, after every legal resource under federal law had been resorted to and had failed to save them, they went to the electric chair.

If the Rosenbergs had been tried and convicted of spying when the war was still on, it is reasonably certain that they would have elicited a good deal of sympathy for believing that the United States ought to share the atom bomb secret with the Soviet Union. It is inconceivable, anyway, that they would have been sentenced to death. Unfortunately for them they were arrested at a time when a majority of opinion in America, liberal as well as conservative, was probably prepared to accept Judge Kaufman's view that the Rosenbergs were responsible for the Korean War, 'with the resultant casualties exceeding 50,000', and, therefore, deserved to die.

There were, of course, always a few people in America who believed in the innocence of the Rosenbergs; but this was a belief never so widely shared as belief in the innocence of Sacco and Vanzetti; and though there has recently been a renewed campaign to prove a miscarriage of justice, this seems unlikely to have more than a very limited effect. While the trial itself was in some ways objectionable, and while it is always possible that the defendants were innocent, there are two main reasons for believing they were guilty. David, it is true, had for some while been on poor terms with Julius, for the latter had fallen behind in payments resulting from an agreement to buy David out of a partnership in a small machine-shop business the two men had started after the war. But was this sufficient motive for him to take such a frightful revenge? Besides, he had (as far as is known) no quarrel with his sister Ethel, and it was quite unnecessary for him to implicate her when he accused Julius. Would he have accused either of them if he had not been satisfied that they could save themselves if they wanted to, as he had done, by confessing? Moreover, the Rosenbergs were a poor, unknown couple; and they lived in a three-room apartment on the lower East Side of New York City, with two small sons dependent on them. They were also Jewish; in other words, they were just the sort of people to attract popular sympathy, if there were any suspicion that they were being persecuted. Why should the F.B.I. have picked on them unless it was genuinely convinced of their guilt?

But in any case the outcry in Europe was not, in the main, a protest against the conviction of the Rosenbergs. It was a demand for clemency, and it was through its refusal to listen to this demand that, paradoxically, the American government allowed Communism a victory. In the case of Sacco and Vanzetti, it didn't matter very much to the Communists what happened. Either they could claim credit for saving two men from a judicial murder or they would be left with two red martyrs. In the case of the Rosenbergs, assuming their guilt, the outcome mattered a great deal. Dead men tell no tales, and while the Rosenbergs lived there was always the risk that they might eventually do what the United States government had vainly tried to frighten them into doing: confess, cooperate, unmask others still active, perhaps, in Soviet espionage. Just as important, regardless of whether they were guilty or innocent, was the effect that such an evidently bloodthirsty execution, if it could be sufficiently publicized, would have on world opinion, particularly on opinion in other democratic countries that looked to the United States for leadership.

The purpose of Communist propaganda, therefore, was to irritate the United States government, to put it into such a defensive position that it could not take the sensible course of sparing the Rosenbergs without the appearance of yielding to outside clamour or admitting to outside charges of duplicity. The Rosenbergs were undoubtedly Communists; and though they were not certainly spies, when they entered the death chamber, they were performing, knowingly or unknowingly, their last and possibly their greatest service to the Party.

3/James Richards and Peter Barnes

Sacco and Vanzetti, though very probably innocent of the murder for which they died in the electric chair, could, as I say, have been guilty of it *if* they had killed from a political motive; if, in other words, they were terrorists, prepared to do murder in order to raise money for their cause.

Terrorism is not, as the younger among us may suppose, a new form of criminal activity that has arisen only recently. It has been with us throughout the present century, and wasn't by any means unknown during the last. Today, however, it appears to be more widespread than it has ever been before, simply because it is being employed by a greater number of people in the hope of furthering a larger variety of causes.

I have deliberately avoided dealing with cases that are less than six years old. And in any event I should think it very rash to guess how many of those more or less contemporary newspaper headline stories of kidnapping or bomb-throwing stand the least chance of being recalled afterwards, for they have followed each other so speedily that the effect has been of one case being drowned out by the next. There is certainly no case from the past six years that one could truthfully name as the outstanding example of modern terrorism, although there very likely will be when one comes to look back on events six years from now. Perhaps the case of Patty Hearst will take pride of place in future volumes of this kind.

I do not know. Nor do I know whether Dr Herrema, the Dutch industrialist who was kidnapped in Ireland in October 1975, is destined to 'live' as one of the victims of modern terrorism. However, I feel sure he deserves to, for in his statement to the press immediately after his release he spoke words that were uniquely wise. Dr Herrema was clearly a man of considerable sensitivity, who had suffered severely at the hands of his kidnappers. Yet he neither hated them nor even wished to see them punished. 'I saw them as children with a lot of problems', he said. 'If they were my own, I would do my utmost to help them.'[37] And since he was able, eventually, to establish a relationship with them, he is just the sort of person who might, in time, have succeeded in reforming them.

Somebody of Dr Herrema's calibre, rather than the executioner, was needed to deal with two members of the Irish Republican Army, which was waging 'war' on England as long ago as 1939–40. This was a war which, while it did not and could not achieve any of its objectives, caused a considerable amount of damage. When Sir Samuel Hoare introduced the government's Prevention of Violence Bill on 24 July 1939 (which gave the Home Secretary approximately the same powers of making deportation orders as those that were given him in 1974), there had already been 127 outrages, most of them in London and the Midlands.

Jim Richards, as he called himself (his real name was M'Cormac or McCormick) was a semi-skilled labourer who arrived in England to be an 'operative officer' near the beginning of the campaign. Nothing is known about his doings until 5 June 1939, when he was in Coventry, lodging with a family that had come to England from Belfast three years before; and on that day he moved with them from Meadow Street to Clara Street. The family consisted of Joseph Hewitt, his wife Mary, his baby daughter and his mother-in-law, Mrs O'Hara. While Joseph Hewitt was working regularly as a tinsmith's mate, Jim Richards, who was just 29, didn't appear to have a job of any kind. Yet he was never without enough money

Bomb Murderers Die at 9 o'clock This Morning

M.P

LAST RITES GIVEN TO DOOMED I.R.A. MEN

EUSTON BOMB VICTIM IN HOSPITAL

THE FOUR CARS IN THE NIGHT

FOUR saloon cars slipped quietly into Winson Green Prison soon after darkness fell last night.

Passers-by noticed nothing unusual, but in them were Phillips, Cross, and the two Pierponts, who are hanging Barnes and Richards to-day.

The only hint was the quickness with which the prison doors opened to take them in.

The "Birmingham Gazette" understands that Barnes and Richards will be hanged at the same moment.

Two executioners will attend each man. The condemned men will see each other just before their deaths.

Last night guards of police and special constables maintained a constant patrol all round the gaol.

Factories, cinemas and public-houses were also especially watched.

Police informed the heads of a factory near the gaol that one of their watchmen was suspect.

But the factory heads were able to vouch for the youth. But it showed the care with which the police guarded against every possible "incident."

There were no scenes outside the prison last night. If anything, the dark streets were more deserted than usual.

But in the nearby public-houses and homes the

One Calm, One Breaks Down as Ring of Police Watch Birmingham Prison All Through Night

WHILE Peter Barnes and James Richards last night received last rites in the condemned cells at Winson Green Prison, Birmingham, from which they are due to go to their execution to-day, efforts were still being made in London to secure four more days for "conclusive proof" of their innocence of the Coventry bomb murders.

As the night wore on the last faint hopes of an eleventh-hour respite were fading. Both men had been told there was no hope. Richards, the "Birmingham Gazette" understands, was calm — as he said at the trial: "I am not afraid to die." But Barnes was in a state of partial collapse.

The men are to be hanged at nine a.m. to-day. They received the last rites of the Roman Catholic Church from Father Collins, one of the priests of St. Patrick's, Dudley-road, not far from the prison.

Even after midnight news of reprieve efforts was still coming in. One of the latest was an appeal signed by prominent

Birmingham Gazette, 7 February 1940

to pay for his board and lodging (23/- a week) and to make occasional visits to the local pub.

Peter Barnes, also a semi-skilled labourer, was 32. He arrived in England much later than Richards, probably near the end of July or the beginning of August, and he spent the first night of his stay in London at 115 Warwick Avenue, where Sarah Keane, a girl whom he had known all his life and was now a domestic servant, was living with her married brother. Barnes's job was to transport 'stuff', such as potassium chlorate, from central sources of supply, mainly Glasgow and Liverpool, to whomever could use it. His mission began very depressingly. The man he had been ordered to meet failed to appear, and he had to spend a whole week in Liverpool—he nearly 'went mad', he wrote[38]—before he at last discovered a contact. Only then was he able to get going.

On 21 August he called on Richards in Coventry, and asked Mrs O'Hara to buy him a long-shaped suitcase. He returned with this to London, where he had now taken a room in Westbourne Terrace. Meanwhile, Richards had, with the help of Hewitt, built a tiny cupboard under the stairs at Clara Street. Richards intended it to be a dump, though it was never actually used as such.

Next day, the first of two mystery men, neither of whom was ever identified, called on Richards. Richards was to describe this man as his boss. He went with him to the Halford Cycle Co., and waited outside while the

Terrorists Strike in West End

I.R.A. BOMBS INJURE 13 IN LONDON

One Woman Gravely Hurt, Others Faint in Street

I.R.A. BOMB EXPLOSIONS WHICH WRECKED SHOP WINDOWS IN OXFORD STREET, LONDON, AND BADLY DAMAGED A CLOAKROOM AT MARBLE ARCH STATION IN THE BLACK-OUT LAST NIGHT INJURED 13 PEOPLE, TWO OF THEM SERIOUSLY

Birmingham Gazette, 23 February 1940

man went in to order a bicycle with a carrier. The cost was £5 19s., and he made a down payment of £5.

On the morning of 24 August the second mystery man appeared at Clara Street. He brought a set of tools with him, and began making the bomb. He came back later to continue with the job, and was there at 7 p.m. when Barnes returned with the suitcase now full of potassium chlorate. Next morning the mystery man finished making the bomb; it was a time bomb. Richards was to swear that he only 'looked on', although a setter for an alarm clock was found in his pocket, and he was to admit quite enough to be convicted of murder. Anyhow, around twelve o'clock, he went off to collect the bicycle, and didn't get back until ten past one. By this time, the man was getting restless, since (as he must have known) the bomb was timed to go off that afternoon.

The man strapped the bomb on to the carrier of his bicycle, and rode off. He got as far as Broadgate, which on this Friday, a market day, was an immensely busy thoroughfare, and he left the bicycle propped up against the pavement kerb, right by Astley's store. Possibly he intended to leave it at a spot near the power station or some other genuinely important target, but since he was aware of the unpredictable behaviour of I.R.A. time bombs, he may have become afraid of riding further.

The bomb exploded at 2.32 p.m. The explosion didn't cause any serious damage to the target, but it gravely injured twelve people and it killed five, including an old man of 81, a boy of 15, and a 21-year-old girl named Elsie Ansell, who was to have been married in two weeks' time. Thus, though it couldn't be described as the most damaging, it was certainly by far the most outrageous incident in the whole year's campaign of terrorism. It was not the first to result in death, but it was the only one in which it proved possible to secure convictions for murder.

On the evening of the same day that the Coventry explosion occurred three men were caught with bombs intended for New Scotland Yard, Westminster Abbey and the Bank of England. Their arrest led the police to Peter Barnes in Westbourne Terrace; and they found on him an unposted letter to a friend in Ireland, which in itself was enough to convict him, for it spoke of his getting back from Coventry late on the previous night (24 August). The police also found in Barnes's possession a quantity of potassium chlorate, and further a receipt for the suitcase.

This led them in time to Clara Street, where they arrested the entire household (except, of course, the baby), and all four of them eventually stood trial for murder at the Birmingham Assizes along with Peter Barnes. The Hewitts and Mrs O'Hara were eventually acquitted, but Barnes and Richards were found guilty and sentenced to death; and if it is ever possible to be certain of guilt, it was so in their case. Richards was only concerned to say in his evidence that it was against I.R.A. orders to kill or risk killing innocent people, and that therefore the explosion, at the time it took place, must have been accidental. But otherwise he was unrepentant: 'My lord', he said after hearing the verdict, 'before you pass sentence, I have something to say. I wish to state my lord, before you pass sentence of death on me, I wish to thank sincerely the gentlemen who have defended me during my trial and I wish to state that the part I took in these explosions since I came to England I have done for a just cause. I say in conclusion, God Bless Ireland and God Bless the men who have fought and died for her. Thank you, my lord.'

Barnes was also unrepentant, but for an entirely different reason. Pale as the corpse he was soon to become, and gripping the edge of the dock, he said in a choked voice: 'I would like to say I am going before my God, as I am condemned to death, I am innocent, and later I am sure it will come out that I had neither hand, act or part in it. That is all I have to say.'[39]

Was that the speech of a coward? It was not a plea for mercy. The same sort of thing was said by Sacco and Vanzetti; and Barnes appeared to be well aware that he had no chance of escaping death. Why, then, should he have so vehemently protested his innocence? Why did he no longer believe, as Richards still believed, that to be guilty was to be right? The question is unanswerable.

Barnes and Richards were executed on 7 February 1940. That morning the Dublin Mansion House Committee, which had been campaigning for the reprieve of the two men, met behind closed blinds. Later they issued a statement saying that England had shown that she cared nothing for Ireland. A number of unemployed (there were many at this period in Ireland's history) marched to Government Buildings carrying a black flag with a skull and crossbones, and a deputation was received by Mr de Valera's private secretary. Meetings of public bodies in Dublin and many other parts of Ireland as well as all football and coursing fixtures for the day were postponed.

But the Irish did not claim, or wish to claim, that either Barnes or Richards was innocent.

PART 3 MURDER

1/H.H. Crippen

If a man were to commit a murder in the hope of winning a kind of immortality for himself, or more crudely of getting his name in the newspaper headlines, the overwhelming chances are that he would be disappointed. For murder, though of course rarer, is not regarded as necessarily more newsworthy than the rest of crime. It must have some special and extraordinary quality to attract the attention of the press and hence of the public.

Opposite: H. H. Crippen and Ethel Le Neve at the Bow Street hearing, 1910

It is hard, if not impossible, to define this quality. Mass murders committed by so-called 'monsters' or 'mad dogs' or (to use the most up-to-date description) 'vicious psychopaths' are reasonably certain to reach the front pages provided there doesn't happen to be any unusual demand on space. On the other hand, if there was ever a murderer who gave the appearance of being normal, and of acting from a perfectly understandable motive, it was Dr Hawley Harvey Crippen, whose name became infamous in 1910.

The sole source of information about Crippen's early life is Crippen himself; and one should remember that at the time he spoke of it he was a liar from necessity. Nevertheless, there is no reason to disbelieve that he was born at Coldwater, Michigan, in 1862, and took a diploma as an ear and eye specialist at the Ophthalmic Hospital, New York, in 1885. From then on until 1896 he was a somewhat peripatetic doctor, practising in various cities throughout the United States. In 1887 he married his first wife Charlotte Bell in Santiago, and he had a son by her, Otto. But Charlotte died in 1890 or 1891 (Crippen was consistently a bit vague about dates), when Otto was hardly more than a baby; and Otto was sent to his paternal grandmother. There is no evidence that he ever saw his father again.

Crippen was back in New York when he met his second wife. She called herself Cora Turner, but her real name was Kunigunde Mackamotzi; her father was Polish and her mother was German. Crippen married her on 1 September 1892, and he was to testify eighteen years later that though she was only 17 she had been living quite openly with a stove manufacturer, which put her (considering the times) more or less in the class of a prostitute. If this was true, he must either have fancied himself Cora's redeemer or he must have fallen passionately in love with her, or both. Sometime after the marriage, he was persuaded by her that she had an exceptionally beautiful singing voice, and he paid for her to have it trained. When he left for London in 1897 to take up an appointment as manager of Munyon's, a business that dealt in the manufacture and sale of patent medicines, he allowed her to stay behind in New York, so that she might continue with her preparations to become a prima donna. Four months later, however, Cora herself was made aware that her voice was unsuited to opera, and she joined Crippen in London. She had decided that her métier was the music hall.

In this belief she apparently remained deceived, despite being hissed off the stage at the Euston Palace of Varieties—one of the few engagements she managed to obtain in almost twelve years of trying. Nevertheless, she adopted a stage name, Belle Elmore; she had friends in the music hall—not with topline names, it's true, but still with engagements—to whom she was known as the 'Bird of Paradise', and eventually she became Hon. Treasurer of the Music Hall Ladies' Guild. Moreover, she lived the part of an artist of her day. She wore furs and jewels and extravagant costumes, all of which, according to Crippen, were paid for by her long-suffering husband.

In November 1899 Crippen went on a business trip to the United States, and was away until the following May. It was during this period that Cora became friendly with Bruce Miller, a fellow-American and a married man, who was in England to try his luck in the music halls. They continued to see each other after Crippen's return, but Miller invariably came to call on Cora in her home when Crippen was out, so that the two of them never met. Eventually, Miller gave up the music hall and returned to America where he became an estate broker in Indiana. Occasionally he wrote to Cora, and one of his letters to her ended 'Love and Kisses to Brown Eyes'. One cannot tell whether their relationship went beyond the bounds of propriety, though one should note that Bruce Miller was to come all the way from Indiana to deny under oath that he had been guilty of misbehaviour. But Crippen was to hold him largely responsible for the misery of his marriage.

The Crippens' social companions, all of them Cora's music hall friends, did not for a moment guess that his marriage was miserable or even quarrelsome. They considered Crippen an unassuming, inoffensive and reserved little man who was obviously devoted to his wife; and they found Cora a vivacious, buxom woman who deserved her husband's admiration. He was to say that though they managed to keep up appearances, actually when they were alone together she nagged him frequently and sometimes flew into rages. Moreover, according to him, it was years since they had slept together, and they occupied separate rooms at their house at 39 Hilldrop Crescent, where they established themselves in 1905.

It is surprising that not one of their social companions ever suspected the little doctor of being unfaithful to his wife, though it is a fair presumption that she must at least have guessed it. He first met Ethel Le Neve in 1901 or in 1902 (again, his vagueness about dates) when she was very young—not more than 21. She had succeeded her sister Nina as a typist at the Drouet Institute, where Crippen was then working. Soon afterwards this business failed, and Crippen went back to Munyon's, and Ethel, as a typist still, went with him. Crippen was to describe the 'love of Ethel' as his 'only happiness', and though he was to say that it was a love which bloomed slowly, it was, on his own admission, in full flower during the last years of his marriage.[40] One recognizes the possibility, therefore, that Crippen's grievance against Bruce Miller did not become important until after his wife had been silenced, and that it was his own affair which was the real cause of disruption.

Still, there is a portrait of Cora painted by one friend, a Mrs Harrison, which shows her to have been a pretty intolerable sort of wife. To begin with, she was paradoxically, in view of her fondness for jewellery and so on, extremely parsimonious. She invariably bought the cheapest foods, and she refused to employ any servants—very unusual in their time for people of the doctor's class. When she and Crippen moved into their Hilldrop Crescent house, she decided she could make a bit of extra money by taking in some German boarders, but even so she wouldn't have a servant, except for a charwoman who came in daily. Crippen had to be up by six to lay the table for breakfast, clean his boarders' boots, and shovel coal before getting off to his office. This experiment didn't last long, which was not surprising, because Cora's dislike of servants had nothing to do with her own superiority as a housekeeper. On the contrary, she was the purest slob.

The Crippens spent most of their time in the kitchen which, if it was ever cleaned, hadn't been on the occasions Mrs Harrison saw it. There were piles of unwashed plates lying around; there were the doctor's unwashed collars littering the table, together with hairpins and parcels of food and other assortments. The gas stove was brown with a combination of rust and cooking stains. And then, by contrast, 'thrown carelessly over a chair was a lovely white chiffon gown embroidered with silk flowers and mounted over white glacé'.[41]

The whole house had an unpleasant, musty smell. This was partly due to the lack of cleaning, partly due to the presence of two cats whom Cora wouldn't allow out, except to be locked in a cage in the garden which she had made Crippen build, but mostly to the fact that she always kept the windows tightly shut. Her intention, apparently, was not so much to keep out the air, as to keep out the cold; and it may be that Crippen approved of this, for he too was an American and used to more sophisticated methods of heating than existed in Britain.

On 31 January 1910 the Crippens entertained Mrs Clara Martinelli and her husband, a retired music hall artist, to dinner at Hilldrop Crescent; and that was the last that any of Cora's friends ever saw of her.

Two days later Ethel Le Neve came to the office of the Music Hall Ladies' Guild at Albion House, Oxford Street, carrying two letters signed 'H.H.C.' on behalf of Cora. One of them was addressed to Miss May, the secretary of the Guild, the other to Cora's fellow members. Both letters said that she had been called away suddenly and urgently to attend a sick relation in California, and that as she didn't expect to be back for several months, she thought it better to resign her position as Hon. Treasurer. A few days later, Crippen called on the Martinellis to explain that as his wife had left at such short notice she'd simply had no time to inform anyone that she was going. However, he felt sure she'd be writing to them, and other friends, as soon as she touched New York.

Towards the end of February, Ethel was seen with Crippen at the Music Hall Ladies' Guild Benevolent Ball, wearing a brooch that seemed remarkably similar to one that belonged to Cora. On 3 March she finally moved into Hilldrop Crescent, nominally as Crippen's housekeeper. Yet there was apparently still no suspicion of her real relationship with him among Cora's friends. She was simply known as the 'typist'. Nor was suspicion awakened when Crippen wrote to Clara and Peter Martinelli on 20 March saying that Cora (or Belle as he now called her) was 'terribly ill with double pneumonia'; and the following morning of 21 March sent a telegram from Victoria Station, where he was on his way with Ethel to spend Easter in Dieppe, telling them that Cora was dead. He made sure that others of her friends would hear the sad news, through paying for a brief notice in the obituary column of the *Era,* which appeared on 26 March.

When he returned from Dieppe, Crippen received many letters of sympathy; and replied to them on black-edged paper. 'I feel sure you will forgive me for my apparent neglect', he wrote to Dr Burroughs, medical adviser to the Guild, 'but I have been almost out of my mind with poor Belle's death so far away.'[42] He didn't, at least not according to his own story, break the news to Ethel until they were back in Hilldrop Crescent, by which time she was already wearing Cora's furs. Ethel's visit to Dieppe had aroused her interest in the French language, and this encouraged Crippen to employ a French maid to help her with her 'housekeeping'.

Perhaps Ethel seemed too much the humble typist for it to enter anyone's head that she could be Crippen's mistress, especially since Crippen made a point of saying in his letters on black-edged paper that he was terribly lonely without Cora and that he intended to get rid of 39 Hilldrop Crescent. To Mrs Martinelli he gave his son's address at 1427 North Hoover Street, Los Angeles, as the place where she should write if she wished to send commiserations; and later he told Mrs Smythson, another member of the Music Hall Ladies' Guild, that his wife had been cremated and her remains were now with him.

Six months passed before things began to go wrong for Crippen. Then Mr and Mrs Nash (whose stage name was Lil Hawthorne) returned from New York, where they'd seen a lot of a Mrs Ginette, who in turn had discovered, after exhaustive inquiries, that no boat had sailed for America on the supposed date of Cora's departure. Accordingly, Mr Nash went to Scotland Yard with this information, which he and Mrs Nash had excitedly carried with them all the way back from New York, and on 9 July Crippen was interviewed by Chief Inspector Dew.

He seemed remarkably calm. He told the Inspector,

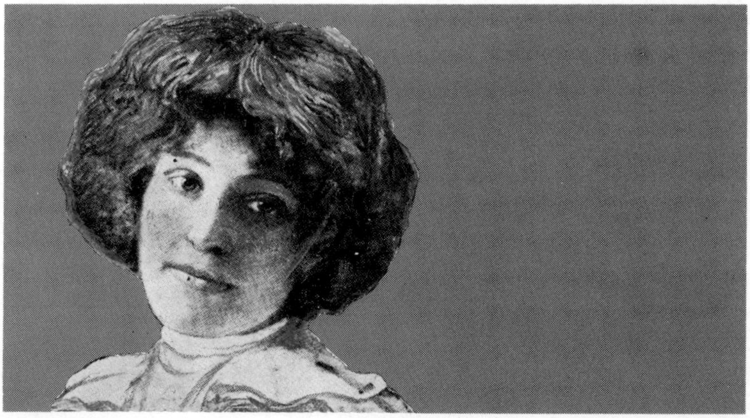

without being pressed, that his whole story of Cora's departure and subsequent demise was a lie designed to cover up a scandal. The fact was she had left him, as she had often threatened to do. There had been a row after the Martinellis left the house on 31 January, because of his failure to conduct Mr Martinelli to the lavatory (though Mr Martinelli knew the way perfectly well), and when he got back from the office next day he found her gone. Dew had no difficulty in believing this story, though he did say he'd need proof that Cora was still alive. Crippen suggested he could advertise for her, and Dew thought this a good idea.

But Crippen's calm had been deceptive. He was unnerved. The very next day, 10 July, he prepared to leave England with Ethel. He asked a Mr Long, who worked for him, to go out and purchase for him a boy's brown suit with accessories. This request was not as startling as it may sound, for Crippen had been in the habit of buying a new outfit for any poor waif who needed it. Later on the same day, Crippen mailed a letter to Mr Long, saying he had gone away and asking him to settle up his household bills, including the French maid's wages.

On 11 July Inspector Dew called at 39 Hilldrop Crescent to find that Crippen and Ethel were gone. This naturally re-aroused his suspicions. He began a thorough search of the premises. He came across a loose brick in the cellar, and this led to the discovery of what lay underneath: a human body, but with the head and all the bones and any evidence of its sex removed. An examination of the stomach showed that death was due to hyoscine poisoning.

According to Crippen, Ethel Le Neve thought it a great lark being dressed as a boy, and that was why she agreed to it. But even if this was true, she was a very poor hand at playing the part of 'Master Robinson', son of Mr Robinson, and it was her studied silence that finally convinced the captain of the vessel bound for Quebec that he had the wanted couple aboard. They were arrested at Father Point, twelve hours' voyage from Quebec, both of them charged with murder, and brought back to London.

Ethel Le Neve was tried separately from Crippen and found not guilty, though it is very hard to believe that this girl who slept with Crippen while he was still living with his wife, who wore Cora's jewels and furs before and after she had (allegedly) been informed of her death, was as innocent of complicity as she pretended to be.

Captain Kendall who identified Crippen aboard the *S.S. Montrose*, as reported in the *News of the World*, 31 July 1910

STOP PRESS

CRIPPEN ARRESTED.

DRAMATIC SCENE ABOARD THE MONTROSE.

FUGITIVES TAKEN INTO CUSTODY AT END OF VOYAGE.

Father Point (Rimouski), July 31.—Crippen and Le Neve have both been identified and arrested.—Reuter.

INSPECTOR DEW BOARDS LINER

Father Point, July 31.

By special arrangement Inspector Dew this morning boarded the steamer Montrose from a rowing boat leaving the numerous newspaper correspondents to follow in the Government tender Eureka.

The object of this proceeding was to enable the detective to make the arrest without perviously arousing the suspicions of "Dr." Crippen and Miss Le Neve.—Reuter.

Mr. Dew was disguised as a pilot.—Central News.

NAL PLANS FOR ARREST.

S FROM LINER SIGNAL CRIPPEN'S SEIZURE.

came tidings of the plans finally e arrest as follows:—

Father Point, July 31.

hours' interruption, indirect with the Montrose via Clark City was restored at evening.

he Montrose was 70 miles t, Captain Kendall telesition was unchanged.

ned Inspector Dew that re becoming increasingly

night Inspector Dew informed en that, owing to the necessity sence of any fuss in connection identification of the suspects, he

Crippen stuck to the story he had told Chief Inspector Dew. It took the jury only a quarter of an hour to find him guilty, and it seems hardly possible to believe they were wrong.

Yet there are puzzling features about the case. To begin with, all that was ever found of Cora's body was flesh and skin that might as well have belonged to a man as a woman. If Crippen was clever enough to dispose of the rest without trace, while he continued to lead his normal life, why did he take the absurd risk of burying the flesh and skin in his cellar? Moreover, it would seem most unlikely that he could have been so resourceful in disposing of the head and bones unless he had thought out in advance what he was going to do with them, or, in other words, unless the murder was premeditated. But there was no suggestion that it was nor any reason why it should have been, unless it was done under growing pressure from Ethel and with her full collaboration.

The fact that he was able to dismember the body so skilfully was, of course, due to his medical training. Marshall Hall, the famous barrister, who in the end refused the case, had a theory that Cora was nymphomaniacal. Crippen admitted to the possession of hyoscine, and Marshall Hall believed that he had given her an overdose in an effort to quieten her, and had been terrified when he realized she was dead. Though this may seem an unlikely theory, Marshall Hall rightly believed that if Crippen were ever to get off, it was his dismemberment of the body, rather than his murder of the woman, that would have to be explained and excused.

But the most extraordinary thing about the case is a letter that Crippen wrote to Ethel Le Neve on the eve of his execution. It is, for the most part, a love letter, which ends with the words, 'Perhaps God will pardon us, because we were like two children in the great unkind world, who clung to one another and gave each other courage.' But in the middle comes a serious protestation of innocence. 'You will remember', he writes, 'that the case for the Crown depended upon the identity which they tried to prove on the piece of flesh and skin, seven inches by six inches. Now, on this piece of skin were two grooves, one as distinctly marked as the other. The medical witnesses for the Crown made no assertion with regard to this piece of skin until they were told that Belle Elmore had had an operation.

'Then they suddenly discovered one groove to be a scar, although admitting the other to be caused by a fold of the skin which had been under great pressure, notwithstanding the undoubted fact that one groove was absolutely continuous with the other in a curved line.

'The medical witnesses for my defence brought forward proof to support their denial that the groove was a scar by demonstrating that there were certain structures present in the so-called scar which could not be present if the mark had resulted from an operation.

'This proof showed so absolutely that the groove was not a scar of an operation that the Crown could only squirm out of their false position by bringing out at the last moment that the presence of these certain structures was to be accounted for by the supposition that the edges of the skin had been turned under and brought together in sewing up the wound of the operation—a most unlikely thing to have been done by skilled surgeons, who especially avoid such an occurrence in abdominal operations . . . it's plain to everyone that if there exists a navel on Belle Elmore's abdomen, the fact that no navel was found on the piece of skin above the so-called scar is proof beyond doubt that the remains found at Hilldrop Crescent were not those of B.E.'[43]

Crippen goes on to say that he is writing 'these things in the hope that the unreliability of the case brought against me may be understood by thoughtful people', but he does not wish Ethel to go to further trouble and expense in collecting evidence. That is hardly to be wondered at considering he had no chance left of escaping the gallows.

But the point is why should he have bothered to protest his innocence to Ethel so elaborately and in a way which a simple typist, if indeed that's what she was, could hardly be expected to understand? Wouldn't it have been enough for him to give her his solemn word that none of the charges made against him was true if that was all he wanted her to believe, or was desperate for her to believe?

Ordinarily, one may be sure it would have been. But Crippen must have been writing in the knowledge that his letter was going to be made public, and he may have convinced himself because he was determined to—such a capacity for fantasizing is not uncommon in a murderer—that the remains at Hilldrop Crescent were not 'B.E.'s', despite overwhelming evidence that they were, including the fact that they were wrapped in his own pyjama top.

But whether he had convinced himself of that or not, if there was one true thing about Crippen, it was his love for Ethel. He would have gone to any length to spare her the same fate that enveloped him.

2/William Podmore

Another British murder which surprisingly excited a lot of attention from the press, for it was not associated with famous names nor was it the work of a 'monster', 'mad dog' or 'vicious psychopath', cost the life of a petty thief named William Podmore.

The reason may be that Vivian Messiter, the victim, was an American who, though he lived most of his adult life abroad, had recently visited his homeland. He arrived in Southampton in September 1928, to work as an agent of the Wolf's Head Oil Company, and took lodgings at 3 Carlton Road, which belonged to a Mr and Mrs Parrott.

Messiter was in his late fifties, and though in his youth he had held a responsible engineering post during the construction of the tunnel under the Hudson River, he wasn't much good as a salesman and the business he was doing was virtually nil. However on 30 October he ordered his breakfast half an hour earlier than usual at 7.30 a.m., explaining that he had an important appointment to keep. Whom this appointment was with will never be known. The evidence showed that it wasn't with Podmore. However, Messiter was not seen at his lodgings again, and two days later Mr Parrott reported his disappearance. Oddly enough, the police were not particularly interested; they assumed that Messiter had returned to America—without bothering to take his luggage with him. As a matter of fact, the police may have had some reason for this suspicion, for the Parrotts found a diary in their lodger's drawer that contained a lover's telegraphic code. Thus 'Bees' stood for 'When do you think you can come?' and 'Cluny' for 'I am awfully lonesome for you'.

The Wolf's Head Oil Company was likewise content to believe that Messiter had simply gone home in a hurry, and more than two months later, on 10 January 1929, a Mr Passmore arrived in Southampton to take his place. When Mr Passmore unlocked the door of the garage at 42 Grove Street, which was to be his headquarters, he found the dead, rotting body of Vivian Messiter. A post mortem examination established that death had been caused by a blow on the head.

William Podmore, who was 28, had arrived in Southampton with his mistress Lily Hambleton on 20 October. He put up in lodgings at 5 Cranbury Avenue until 2 November. He called himself William F. Thomas, which was prudent of him since he was wanted in his own name by the Manchester police. He had been a petty crook since the age of 11, though he had never been guilty of an act of violence (or at least had never been charged with one). He answered an advertisement which Messiter had placed in the *Southampton Echo* asking for an assistant, and there is no doubt he was hired. There is no doubt either that he cheated Messiter by pretending to have made oil sales to companies which didn't exist, and no doubt finally that he met Messiter at his garage on 30 October, though this was not the important appointment to which Messiter was referring when he asked for an early breakfast.

But Podmore was not accused of murder until nearly a year after he had made a statement (which he stuck to at his trial) and after he had served two prison sentences for fraud. Moreover, it was only by a majority that the magistrates agreed to commit him; and at the trial itself, while the Lord Chief Justice was clearly against him, the prosecution felt it necessary to boost their case by calling two prisoners, both of them with bad criminal records, who related damaging admissions that Podmore had allegedly made to them.

The prosecution did not suggest that the crime was premeditated. Their theory—and it was in reality no more than a theory, however convincing—was that Messiter had discovered Podmore was cheating him, had threatened to go immediately to the police, and that Podmore in a sudden uncontrollable fit of rage had killed him. This may possibly have been true, though no evidence at all was produced to show that Podmore was given to rages. It was, however, unfortunate for him that in the story he told before he knew exactly what was the case against him he referred to a mysterious third party—an agent, he said—who might have done the murder. This, so the prosecution alleged, was why he deliberately left a receipt dated 30 October in the dead man's coat pocket, hoping it would be found there. But the receipt was for a two shillings and sixpence commission on the sale of oil and had, in fact, been collected by Messiter the day before from H. F. Galton, a foreman on the Southern Railway. It was improperly dated.

Still, this apart, the evidence against Podmore—and all of it was circumstantial—was just as consistent with an attempt to cover up fraud as with one to cover up murder. Moreover, there was circumstantial evidence that told in his favour. The murder weapon, a hammer, which was found in the garage, was claimed by a Mr

The garage at Southampton where the body of Vivian Messiter lay for two months before being discovered

Marsh, an engineer. He said he had lent it to a stranger, but failed to pick out Podmore at an identification parade, nor did his description of the borrower at the trial fit the defendant in the dock. Mr Card, a grocer, swore he had seen the same young man with Messiter both on 30 October and a fortnight before, that is before Podmore and Lil arrived in Southampton. The police, who examined Podmore's clothes, failed to find the least sign of bloodstains; nor were they able to trace any of Messiter's personal belongings which Podmore was alleged to have stolen. And, for an unpremeditated murder, it must have been astonishingly cold-blooded. Not only did Podmore take his time afterwards to destroy evidence that would implicate him, but having done this calmly drove in Messiter's car to Downton (near Salisbury), where he was interviewed by another potential employer, and that same evening went to the theatre with Lil to see *Paddy The Next Best Thing*.

In the circumstances, there was understandably a good

deal of public pressure brought to bear on the Labour Home Secretary, Mr Clynes, to commute Podmore's sentence from death to life imprisonment. Mr Clynes refused on the grounds that his personal dislike of capital punishment was grounds in itself for not interfering with the decision of the jury and the belief of the judge. He was much praised for his courage, though one may think that in a case of such dubiety he would have shown considerably greater courage had he taken the opposite course.

Podmore went to the gallows still protesting his innocence. That may have meant everything—or nothing. He was a poorly educated man of above average intelligence, rather arrogant, and with a remarkable memory, as he revealed several times during his cross-examination by Sir Thomas Inskip. But someone murdered Vivian Messiter. And if it wasn't Podmore, who was it? There was no other candidate in view, which in the last analysis is why he died.

Below left: *Daily Mirror,* 4 February 1930 and (right) *Daily Mirror,* 10 March 1930

'SCORNED LOVE' IN MURDER CHARGE

C.I.D. Inspector's Evidence at Garage Hearing

PODMORE FOR TRIAL

Committed by Majority After a Fifteen-Day Hearing

After a hearing that had lasted fifteen days the Southampton magistrates yesterday decided by a majority to send William Henry Podmore for trial on the charge of murdering Vivian Messiter in a garage.

Inside the court it was a day of drama. Under cross-examination, Inspector Prothero, of Scotland Yard, admitted that several people besides Podmore had been suspected of committing the crime.

A man had said a woman came home covered with blood. "Jealousy and love scorned were at the bottom of that," declared the inspector emphatically.

For the defence Mr. O'Connor submitted that no jury would convict Podmore and that the prosecution facts were a "mass of rubbish."

STRUGGLE WITH POLICE

Women's Screams and Cries Heard in Court Room—Dramatic Scene

PODMORE'S LIFE OF CRIME

Housebreaking When He Was Only Nine Years Old

DEATH SENTENCE

Dramatic Court Scene—'I Know Nothing of Garage Murder'

"I still repeat I know nothing whatever about it."

So said William Henry Podmore, "the man with the scar," in the dock at Winchester Assizes on Saturday, before he was sentenced to death for the Southampton garage murder.

Over sixteen months have passed since the murder was committed.

It was two months later before the body of Vivian Messiter, the oil agent, was found in his garage, and from that day the police have worked unremittingly to build up the case against Podmore.

There were dramatic scenes when the end of the trial came. Amid a tense silence the jury, after an absence of eighty-three minutes, filed back into the court.

The word "guilty" came clearly from the lips of the foreman. Some women raised their handkerchiefs to their eyes.

Podmore stood like a statue in the dock. The short figure in a blue suit with a coloured handkerchief peeping out of his breast pocket seemed dazed and dumb.

After Podmore's words the Lord Chief Justice, in a low voice, pronounced the death sentence.

3/Albert Fish, Ian Brady and Myra Hindley, Landru, Neville Heath, John George Haigh and others

Horrific murders may be monstrous, but their perpetrators are not by definition monsters. They are human beings. Some of them are good-looking human beings. Some of them have charm.

It would surely be logical to suppose that a type of crime which a normal person rightly believes he could never, under any circumstances, even be tempted to commit would automatically lead him to consider a person who did commit it so grossly abnormal as to be incapable of responding to punishment or deserving of it. But the opposite is true. The more horrific a murder the greater the general desire to see its perpetrator punished as severely as, or more severely than, the law permits.

This is no doubt due, in part, to a terror of the unthinkable, but it is none the less perverse for that. A prime example is afforded by the notorious case of Albert Fish, which is excellently described by Dr Fredric Wertham in his book *The Show of Violence*.[44] In 1928, Albert Fish, who was a mild-mannered man approaching 60 and the father of six children, called at the home of a Mr and Mrs Budd in New York on the pretext of offering their son a job. The Budds also had a daughter, Grace, who was aged 10. Fish said he would like to take Grace to a children's birthday party which his sister was giving, and the Budds, a little hesitantly, consented.

They never saw her again. But six years later they received an unsigned letter, which read in part: '. . . I came to your flat on the third of June, 1928, and under the pretense of taking your daughter Grace to a party at my sister's I took her up to Westchester County, Worthington, to an empty house up there, and I choked her to death. I cut her up and ate part of her flesh.'[45]

This letter was eventually traced back to Fish, and provided an accurate account of what he had done. He subsequently elaborated it in six signed confessions and in statements to Dr Wertham. He said he had cut off Grace's head before dismembering the body; he had taken parts of the body home with him, had cooked them in various ways with carrots and onions and strips of bacon, and had eaten them over a period of nine days.

That was not all. There was, according to Dr Wertham, no known perversion that Fish had not indulged in. He had eaten his own excrement; he had put pieces of cotton, saturated with alcohol, up his rectum and set fire to them; he had, over a period of years, stuck needles into his body in the region of his genitals, and a series of x-ray photographs by Dr Wertham showed that twenty-nine of these needles—some eroded with rust—were still lodged in him.

Opposite: Albert Fish, multi-murderer and cannibal; he was executed in New York in 1928

Opposite: Ian Brady and Myra Hindley and (below) the house in which they lived in Hattersley, Cheshire, where Edward Evans's body was found

In pursuit of his sado-masochistic pleasures he had molested at least a hundred children. Nor had Grace Budd presented him with his first or only chance to practise cannibalism. Estimates, after his arrest, of other child murders he had committed ranged from five to fifteen. Finally, Fish was what is commonly called a 'religious maniac'. For the past ten years, he had been suffering from auditory hallucinations; voices had been urging him to new feats of atonement.

Dr Wertham diagnosed Fish's condition as a 'paranoid psychosis', or, in other words, believed that Fish was legally insane—that he did not know that what he was doing was wrong. But there were psychiatrists to take the opposite view for the prosecution, and in the end the public got what they wanted, and Fish went to the electric chair. Subsequently, it came out that though a majority of the jury who condemned Fish to death believed that he was legally insane, they decided he ought to be executed anyhow!

Another example of this same perversity—the desire to see those most severely punished for whom, among all offenders, punishment is least appropriate—is provided by the so-called Moors Murders. In that case, the two culprits, Ian Brady and Myra Hindley, were put on trial in 1966, a year after capital punishment had been abolished in Britain. They were sentenced to life imprisonment, which can be, and very probably will be in this case, interpreted to mean just that. They would undoubtedly have been executed, as the great majority of people wished, if the death penalty had still been in force.

The issue of their mental state was not in dispute, because they preferred not to raise it. But one may suggest that whether they were sane or insane, mad or bad, sick or evil, should have ultimately made no difference to the way they were treated. If there is any justification for punishing people, one must be certain that they have the capacity to resist the urge to do wrong. Even granted that that question is answerable in the case of a reasonably common temptation, it is, surely, unanswerable by any of us, including psychiatrists and judges, when the temptation is unimaginable.

How many of us, including psychiatrists and judges, can imagine ourselves wishing to do what Ian Brady and Myra Hindley did (though some people consider that Myra Hindley was not an actual participant in the murders)? They were living together at 16 Wardle Brook Avenue, Hattersley, in Cheshire. He was 27, she was 23; he held a job as a stock clerk at Milwards in West Gorton,

Following pages: Aerial view of police conferring beside John Kilbride's grave

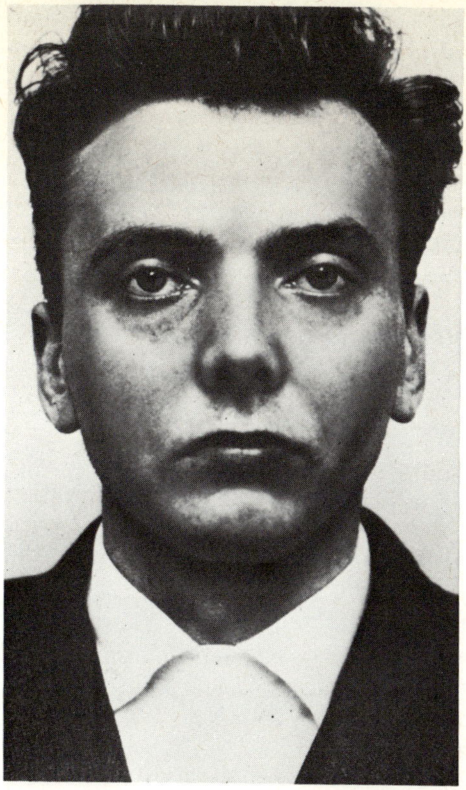

she was a typist in the same firm, and they both looked their parts. Some time between 23 November 1963 and 7 October 1965, Ian Brady murdered John Kilbride, aged 12, and Myra was an accessory after the fact. On 26 December they tortured and killed Leslie Ann Downey, aged 10. Brady took photographs of this child in indecent postures, and he made a tape recording while they were being taken of the child's agony and of his own and Myra's brutalities. These were to be important evidence against them. But that was the last thing Brady worried about at the time. Presumably he wanted a permanent record of his handiwork which he and Myra could luxuriate in whenever they felt like it. Finally, on or about 7 October 1965, Brady beat and murdered Edward Evans, aged 17.

The bodies of John Kilbride and Leslie Ann Downey were discovered where Brady had buried them on the moors. The body of Edward Evans was awaiting a similar burial when the police arrived at 16 Wardle Brook Avenue. They found it trussed up in a blanket in Myra's bedroom. It had an electric-light cable pulled tightly round its neck, and it had been horribly mangled by thirteen blows with an axe.

In some ways, this case is comparable with the kidnapping and murder of a six-year-old child in Kansas named Bobby Greenlease; and also with the case of the Lonely Hearts Murderers in New York (Fernandez and Beck) and other instances of *folie à deux,* where the male partner had a record of delinquency while the female was besotted with love for him, but was not previously criminal. The Moors Murders, however, are distinguished from these both by the nature and the degree of their monstrousness, which was associated with, though not explained by, extreme sadistic and pornographic impulses. Obviously, Ian Brady and Myra Hindley could not have been left at large, but they might have told us a lot which we need to know about the causes, the basic causes, which led (or impelled) them to commit such appalling crimes. And we might in turn have eventually found a way to make it safe for society were they to live in freedom.

Nor would this all be a matter for psychiatry, whose importance in dealing with crime has, perhaps, been exaggerated. Maurice Richardson wrote in the *Observer* of Brady: 'He probably drew something sinister in the chromosal lottery'.[46] Maybe he did; and maybe we could ascertain what precisely that was; and maybe we could discover that it needn't be a lottery at all.

As it is, we have simply put these two twisted human beings in prison, as far as Brady is concerned presumably until he is dead. It might have been, in fact it would have been, more merciful to kill him; and though it was very understandable to say that neither deserved mercy, such an emotional response to what they did was unhelpful. For, in fact, the abolition of capital punishment offers a real chance to unearth the hidden causes of horrific murder, though it is a chance that up to now has been totally wasted.

Would we, for example, be in a better position to explain Landru, the French bluebeard, if he had been imprisoned for life instead of executed? One doubts it, especially since, like Crippen, he resolutely denied his guilt and agreed only reluctantly to an appeal for mercy to the President with the remark 'but why should an innocent man ask for pardon?'[47]

There was no hint of trouble in Landru's home background, which was poor but respectable and loving. Yet from earliest manhood he was a fraud, and later murdered ten of the 283 women with whom he is said to have had relations. He was the model for Charlie Chaplin's film *Monsieur Verdoux*—and Chaplin does offer an explanation of his behaviour—but that is fiction, not fact. The real Landru remains inexplicable.

The same observation applies to other horrific murders which were tried in England before the abolition of capital punishment. Neville Heath, for instance, was, like Landru, delinquent from the outset of his career. At the age of 20, in July 1938, he was sent to Borstal. He was released after less than a year 'owing to the national emergency', joined up in the Royal Army Service Corps, soon got a commission, and was posted to the Middle East in 1940, with the acting rank of captain. But, just over a year later, he was court-martialled for various dishonesties, cashiered and sent home on a troopship.

He jumped ship at Durban and made his way to Johannesburg, where he passed himself off as Captain Selway, M.C., of the Argyll and Sutherland Highlanders. Later, in December 1941, he changed his name to Armstrong and joined the South African Air Force as a private. Again, it took him a very short time to get his commission, and though the South African authorities did eventually find out about his past, they decided to give him a chance to rehabilitate himself. Their faith seemed justified. In 1944, he was seconded to the Royal Air Force, and remained with it until after D-Day. But on 5 December he found himself once more in trouble.

Below: Police remove the clothing of Doreen Marshall, Neville Heath's second victim, from Bournemouth beach (opposite)

He was court-martialled on six charges; three of conduct prejudicial to good order and military discipline; three of wearing military decorations without authority. He was cashiered for the second time.

Meanwhile, he had married in 1942 while he was still in South Africa, and had since been divorced. His estranged wife revealed, unintentionally, that all his delinquencies were symptomatic of a longing to rise above his lower middle class background, when she was reported as saying in an interview with a South African paper after his conviction for murder: 'At the moment my heart goes out in sympathy to his family. I never knew they existed, for he told me he was alone in the world, the only son of the late Mr and Mrs P. J. Armstrong of Melton Hall, Woodbridge, Suffolk, England.'[48] Melton Hall was clearly a corruption of Merton Hall

Road, where his parents actually lived in Wimbledon; Woodbridge is, in fact, the nearest town to the Hollesley Bay Colony—the Borstal he attended; and as the *only* son (he had, in reality, a younger brother) of the *late* Mr and Mrs P. J. Armstrong he killed off his entire family!

Still, a longing to rise above one's background is not uncommon, and can be, and usually is, achieved by more constructive means than Heath used. To say that Heath was delinquent from social ambition is true only as far as it goes, and inevitably leaves the question of why unanswered.

Similarly, the fact that Heath was a sadist is not a sufficient explanation of the monstrosity of his murders. The one with which he was charged and of which he was convicted took place at the Pembridge Court Hotel in the early hours of 21 June 1946. Heath entered this small

hotel, where there was no night porter and where he was already in occupation of room 4, with Mrs Marjory Gardner at about midnight. Heath left unnoticed in the morning with his luggage but with his bill unpaid.

At two o'clock in the afternoon of the same day a chambermaid entered his room. Mrs Gardner was lying on one of the two beds. She was naked and dead. Her ankles were tightly bound together by a handkerchief; marks on her wrists indicated that these had been similarly bound, though they were now free. There was evidence that blood had been washed from her face, and that she had been moved from one bed to the other before or after death. On the front and back of her body, and about her head, were the marks of seventeen lashes. These had been administered with some kind of steel woven thong. Her nipples were nearly bitten off. There was free bleeding from the vagina, from the entrance of the passage to the womb. This was due to a seven-inch long tear of the interior of the vagina. The wound might conceivably have been inflicted with the ferrulelike tip of the thong.

The second murder, to which Heath confessed and which he authorized his counsel to bring up, took place some time after midnight on 27 June 1946, on the Bournemouth beach. The victim was a Miss Doreen Marshall whom Heath had met the day before, while staying at the Tollard Royal Hotel, registered in the name of Rupert Brooke. Miss Marshall's body was discovered on the evening of 8 July, by which time Heath had been charged with Mrs Gardner's murder. It was naked, except for a shoe on the left foot, but clothing had been put on top of it, and it was concealed in a kind of tunnel behind some rhododendrons, with a fir bough at the entrance. Miss Marshall had not been thrashed, as Mrs Gardner had been. But there was evidence that she also had had her wrists bound. Before she died her assailant had knelt on her and crushed her ribs. He had slashed her throat with a knife and finally cut it, which was the cause of death. Afterwards, he had bitten her nipples right off and inflicted other mutilations far more savage and obscene than those that had desecrated Mrs Gardner.

Heath pleaded insanity, and sat through his trial with an air of complete indifference, as though, to use one of his own favourite R.A.F. expressions, he 'couldn't care less'. Indifference is no doubt what he actually felt. There was at any rate no truth whatever in the rumour, which subsequently got into print, that the 'monster' had murdered Miss Marshall in order to bolster his insanity plea. Heath himself, as his own counsel has said, was most reluctant to plead insane and consented only out of consideration for his parents.

Besides, the only issue fought between a psychiatrist for the defence and two doctors without psychiatric qualifications for the prosecution was whether or not Heath was *legally* insane under the M'Naghten Rules (the plea of diminished responsibility for murder, which Heath must surely have won, had he been both willing and able to use it, was not introduced until 1957). 'They are still good rules', said Mr Anthony Hawke, leading Crown Counsel, 'inasmuch as they place some limit on irresponsibility for crime . . . As I say—and I repeat—that this man is abnormal nobody denies and nobody seeks to contest. If you come to the conclusion that his is an abnormality which, in the course of the satisfaction of it, involves grievous bodily harm to the victim of his

Neville Heath on his way to court

satisfaction and that grievous bodily harm ends in the victim's death, then the mere fact that his is an abnormal mind does not excuse him from the responsibility, the awful responsibility, that he has taken in removing a person's life.'[49]

Neither the psychiatrist for the defence nor the doctors for the prosecution had found out much about Heath; and since they all appeared to agree in the end that he was legally sane, he was convicted and sentenced to death. The Home Secretary appointed a panel of psychiatrists to examine Heath after the trial. These psychiatrists were not bound by the M'Naghten Rules, but they nevertheless passed Heath as fit for hanging, and on 26 October 1946 he was executed at Pentonville prison. No sensible person could have doubted that sooner or later another man of Heath's misshapen kind would come and that when he did he neither would nor could be deterred by what had been done to this one.

In fact, he appeared three years later in the person of John George Haigh, whose crimes were, if anything, even more horrific than Heath's.

Haigh would probably have been executed even if he had been permitted to plead diminished responsibility instead of insanity, for the prosecution was not prepared to admit that he was mentally abnormal, but pictured him as a mere scoundrel who was hoping to get to Broadmoor by pretending to be insane. He belonged to a somewhat higher class than Heath, but his upbringing had been very strict and Biblicist. He, too, was in revolt against it, though that, again, could be true of a great many others who feel no compulsion to kill or even cheat. He had a criminal record at the time of his arrest for murder, and this was considerably worse than Heath's. He first went to prison in 1935, at the age of 24, after he had been given fifteen months for fraud and forgery. Between 1938 and 1947 he was twice sentenced for similar offences, on the first occasion for four years and on the second for twenty-one months.

During his periods of freedom, he gave evidence of his 'rehabilitation' by committing, on his own count, nine murders. The police, however, were able to confirm only six of them, since he either could not remember or never knew the names of three of his supposed victims. He dissolved the bodies of all the people he killed in a tank of sulphuric acid.

In February 1949 Haigh was staying at the Onslow Court Hotel, a small residential hotel in South Kensington, where he met an old lady named Mrs Olive Durand-

Deacon, who confided to him her idea for marketing artificial fingernails. Haigh said there was a firm in Crawley, called Hurstlea Products, of which he was a director and which might well be interested in such a plan. He suggested they should go there together and try to interest the managing director. Crawley happened to be the place where Haigh had a storehouse which was convenient for keeping a tank of acid.

Mrs Deacon-Durand's disappearance caused quite a stir at the Onslow Court Hotel, and Haigh told her bosom friend Mrs Lane that though he had arranged to drive Mrs Deacon-Durand to Crawley, she had failed to keep the appointment, and he had gone there on his own. He volunteered to accompany Mrs Lane to the police, and he told them the same story as he had told her. Yet, if he was really the appallingly cunning scoundrel he was to be painted, he must surely have realized that the police would check up on him, as of course they did. When they found he had a criminal record they instituted immediate inquiries in Crawley, whither he and Mrs Lane had led them.

They found out he was not a director of Hurstlea Products, though the company had loaned him a storehouse in return for work he was supposed to be doing on their behalf in London. They forced an entry into the storehouse. There they found a revolver, gallons of acid, a rubber apron and rubber gloves, and splashes of blood on the walls. They also found a receipt for a Persian lamb coat, which had been left at a cleaner's in Horsham. Later they discovered that the jewellery belonging to Mrs Deacon-Durand had been sold in Horsham by a man identified as Haigh from a photograph.

When he was confronted with this evidence, Haigh confessed with apparent relish. He had, he said, shot Mrs Deacon-Durand in the back of the head. Then he made an incision on one side of her throat, filled a glass with her blood, and drank it. Finally, after depriving her of her fur coat and her jewellery, he put her remains in a 45-gallon tank, which he filled with sulphuric acid.

Haigh went on to tell his whole story, or (as the police suspected) more than there really was of it. The idea of dissolving the bodies in acid had come to him by chance after the very first murder he had committed. That was in 1943, when he killed Donald McSwann, a young man whom he had promised to help avoid the call-up, by hitting him over the head with an iron bar in the basement of 79 Gloucester Road, London, where he was living at the time. He immediately satisfied his thirst for a draught

Daily Express, 4 March 1949

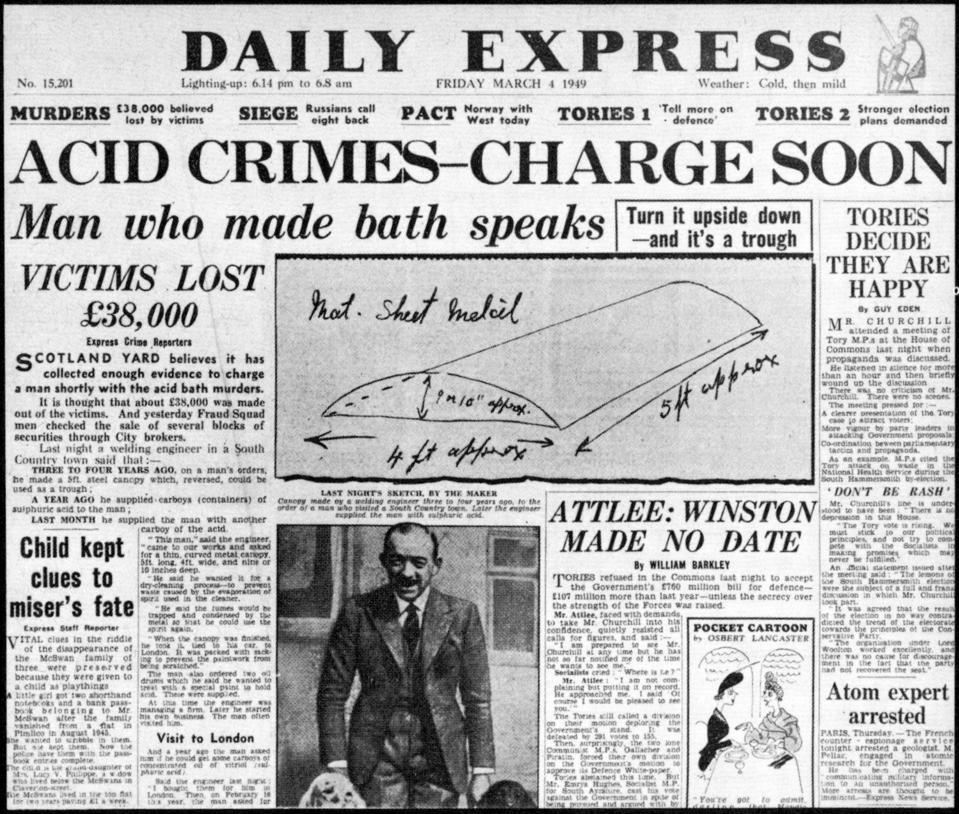

DAILY EXPRESS

No. 15,201 Lighting-up: 6.14 pm to 6.8 am FRIDAY MARCH 4 1949 Weather: Cold, then mild

MURDERS £38,000 believed lost by victims **SIEGE** Russians call eight back **PACT** Norway with West today **TORIES 1** 'Tell more on defence' **TORIES 2** Stronger election plans demanded

ACID CRIMES–CHARGE SOON

Man who made bath speaks

Turn it upside down —and it's a trough

VICTIMS LOST £38,000

Express Crime Reporters

SCOTLAND YARD believes it has collected enough evidence to charge a man shortly with the acid bath murders.

It is thought that about £38,000 was made out of the victims. And yesterday Fraud Squad men checked the sale of several blocks of securities through City brokers.

Last night a welding engineer in a South Country town said that:—

THREE TO FOUR YEARS AGO, on a man's orders, he made a 5ft. steel canopy which, reversed, could be used as a trough;

A YEAR AGO he supplied carboys (containers) of sulphuric acid to the man;

LAST MONTH he supplied the man with another carboy of the acid.

"This man," said the engineer, "came to our works and asked for a thin, curved metal canopy, 5ft. long, 4ft. wide, and nine or 10 inches deep.

"He said he wanted it for a dry-cleaning process—to prevent waste caused by the evaporation of spirit used in the cleaner.

"He said the fumes would be trapped and condensed by the metal so that he could use the spirit again.

"When the canopy was finished, he took it, tied to his car, to London. It was packed with sacking to prevent the paintwork from being scratched."

The man also ordered two oil drums which he said he wanted to treat with a special paint to hold acid. These were supplied.

At this time the engineer was managing a firm. Later he started his own business. The man often visited him.

Visit to London

And a year ago the man asked him if he could get some carboys of concentrated oil of vitriol (sulphuric acid).

Said the engineer last night: "I bought them for him in London. Then, on February 16 this year, the man asked for

LAST NIGHT'S SKETCH, BY THE MAKER

Canopy made by a welding engineer three to four years ago, to the order of a man who visited a South Country town. Later the engineer supplied the man with sulphuric acid.

Child kept clues to miser's fate

Express Staff Reporter

VITAL clues in the riddle of the disappearance of the McSwan family of three were preserved because they were given to a child as playthings

A little girl got two shorthand notebooks and a bank passbook belonging to Mr. McSwan after the family vanished from a flat in Pimlico in August 1945.

She wanted to scribble in them. But she kept them. Now the police have them with the passbook entries complete.

The child is the grand-daughter of Mrs. Lucy V. Philippe, a widow who lived below the McSwans in Claverton-street.

The McSwans lived in the top flat for two years paying £1 a week.

ATTLEE: WINSTON MADE NO DATE

By WILLIAM BARKLEY

TORIES refused in the Commons last night to accept the Government's £760 million bill for defence—£107 million more than last year—unless the secrecy over the strength of the Forces was raised.

Mr. Attlee, faced with demands to take Mr. Churchill into his confidence, quietly resisted all calls for figures, and said:—

"I am prepared to see Mr. Churchill at any time but he has not so far notified me of the time he wants to see me."

Socialists cried: "Where is he?"

Mr. Attlee: "I am not complaining but putting it on record. He approached me. I said 'Of course I would be pleased to see you.'"

The Tories still called a division on their motion deploring the Government's stand. It was defeated by 291 votes to 155.

Then, surprisingly, the two lone Communist M.P.s Gallacher and Piratin, forced their own division on the Government's motion to approve its Defence White-paper.

Tories abstained this time. But Mr. Emrys Hughes, Socialist M.P. for South Ayrshire, cast his vote against the Government in spite of being pursued and argued with by

POCKET CARTOON
by OSBERT LANCASTER

"You've got to admit,

TORIES DECIDE THEY ARE HAPPY

By GUY EDEN

MR. CHURCHILL attended a meeting of Tory M.P.s at the House of Commons last night when propaganda was discussed.

He listened in silence for more than an hour and then briefly wound up the discussion.

There was no criticism of Mr. Churchill. There were no scenes.

The meeting pressed for:—

A clearer presentation of the Tory case to attract voters;

More vigour by party leaders in attacking Government proposals;

Co-ordination between parliamentary tactics and propaganda.

As an example, M.P.s cited the Tory attack on waste in the National Health Service during the South Hammersmith by-election.

'DON'T BE RASH'

Mr. Churchill's line is understood to have been: "There is no depression in this House.

"The Tory vote is rising. We must stick to our political principles, and not try to compete with the Socialists in making promises which may never be fulfilled."

An official statement issued after the meeting said: "The lessons of the South Hammersmith election were the subject of a full and frank discussion in which Mr. Churchill took part.

"It was agreed that the result of the election in no way contradicted the trend of the electorate towards the principles of the Conservative Party.

"The organisation under Lord Woolton worked excellently, and there was no cause for discouragement in the fact that the party had not recovered the seat."

Atom expert arrested

PARIS, Thursday.—The French counter-espionage service tonight arrested a geologist, M. Peliar, engaged in atomic research for the Government.

He has been charged with "communicating military information to an unauthorised person." More arrests are thought to be imminent.—Express News Service.

Gathering evidence from Haigh's storehouse in Crawley Right: Haigh as 12-year-old choirboy

Opposite: Haigh arriving at Horsham Magistrate's Court, 1 April 1949

of his victim's blood, but then found himself without an idea of what he was going to do with the body. In fact (so he said) he let it lie where it had fallen for a whole day until he suddenly hit on the notion of disposing of it with acid. He poured the sludge down a manhole in the basement.

Haigh was tried for the murder of Mrs Deacon-Durand in July 1949. Like Heath, he pleaded insanity, though evidently without reluctance, and authorized his counsel to refer to all the other bodies dissolved in acid for which he claimed to have been responsible. The prosecution readily believed those parts of his confession which suited their case, and rejected the rest. Dr Yellowlees appeared as the only witness for the defence. His case largely depended on Haigh's own story that every so often he suffered from an irresistible urge to drink blood, occasioned by a recurrent nightmare that began with an image of a forest of crucifixes. The prosecution had no difficulty in getting this theory laughed out of court, especially since Haigh had been unwise enough to ask one of the police officers who interrogated him what were the chances of anyone being released from Broadmoor mental hospital.

But though the prosecution naturally made a great point of this, the fact that a man in Haigh's situation should have asked such a question of a police officer was surely evidence in itself either of idiocy (and Haigh was certainly no idiot) or of a grave imbalance of mind. And although Dr Yellowlees conceded under cross-examination that his patient might have fooled him, doesn't the alternative theory that Haigh acted merely from a motive of greed seem even less credible? Doesn't it in truth seem quite incredible?

From Mrs Deacon-Durand he got little more than Heath got from killing Miss Doreen Marshall (Heath got a watch, a brooch and the return half of a first-class London–Bournemouth ticket) and it was never suggested that Heath murdered for gain. Besides, it cost Heath nothing to mutilate Doreen Marshall; it must have cost Haigh something to dispose of Mrs Deacon-Durand.

It is true that Haigh did profit by a good many thousands of pounds from others of his victims. This was due to his expertise in forgery, for which he went to prison on three occasions and which he revered and practised as an art. According to his own account, he kept the McSwann parents happy for a whole year by writing them letters which they were fully satisfied came from their son, though he finally killed them both by the same method and in the same place as he had killed him. There is no doubt that he managed, through forgery of letters, to persuade Rose Kennedy's brother that she and her husband were about to leave for South Africa after he had actually turned their bodies into sludge in his storehouse at Crawley; and, further, to convince the brother that he had lent Dr Archie Henderson £2,500 and was to be given his house and car if the money were not repaid within two months.

Yet apparently he had next to nothing left a year later—a cheque that he had given to the manageress of the Onslow Court Hotel bounced—when he met Mrs Deacon-Durand, from whom he stood to gain so little. Nor did he bother to make sure the sludge was free of tell-tale signs. He simply emptied it in the yard outside his storehouse, and the police found in it human fat, undissolved bone, a denture, and a red plastic bag that had belonged to Mrs Deacon-Durand.

It is, indeed, possible that if the police hadn't found these things—and Haigh could very easily have got rid of them if he'd wanted to—they would have disbelieved his entire confession. For, once again, this was a crime beyond belief. It certainly could not be explained in the terms that were eventually used to explain it, and that satisfied the jury. Within a matter of seventeen minutes Haigh was found guilty, and sentenced to death.

He had it in common with many famous criminals, murderers or not, that he was inordinately vain: vain not only about his outstanding brilliance as a forger and his unique method of disposing of bodies, but about other things, including his knowledge of classical music. It is said that while he was awaiting execution, he asked, though his request was refused, for a piano to be placed in his cell so that he might give his guards a practical demonstration of what he was trying to teach them. It is also said that he was most anxious about the appearance he would make in the Chamber of Horrors at Madame Tussaud's waxworks, and to make sure it would be as good as possible bequeathed them his wardrobe!

There is no evidence that he was in the least afraid to die, though he wanted a rehearsal of the hanging before the actual event in case anything went wrong on the day! One must assume that if there had been no capital punishment in 1949, and Haigh were still alive, he would now (1976) be rotting in prison at the age of 65. He would be considered (quite likely rightly) too dangerous to release, but nothing would have been done to discover the underlying causes of the dangerousness in him.

4/Charles Manson

The Manson case belongs in the category of horrific murders, but it also (up to the present) stands on its own.

At midnight on 9 August 1969 the home of Sharon Tate, the film actress, above the Hollywood hills, was invaded by four unwelcome young strangers. One of them, Linda Kasabian, was to deny any active part in the proceedings that followed and to testify against her confederates. The other three, Susan Atkins, 21, Patricia Krenkwinkel, also 21, and Charles Watson, 23, murdered the pregnant Sharon Tate and four of her friends with unbridled brutality and apparent enjoyment. On the following night, they were joined by Leslie Van Houten, 20, in the no less savage and (for them) thrilling annihilation of Leno LaBianca, owner of a chain of Los Angeles grocery stores, and his wife Rosemary. The four murderers and Linda Kasabian were members of a hippie colony or 'Family' whose 'father' was a 34-year-old prisoner on parole named Charles Manson. Manson believed himself to be Jesus Christ, or at any rate encouraged his children to believe that he was, and his word was their law. He had commanded them to kill.

Manson, Susan Atkins, Patricia Krenkwinkel and Leslie Van Houten stood trial together, while Watson, who succeeded in evading extradition from Texas for over a year, was tried separately after his return to California. Under Californian practice, there is one trial to establish the fact of guilt (or innocence), and in the case of a conviction for first degree murder a second trial to enable the jury to recommend whether the penalty should be death or life imprisonment. In this case, all five defendants were convicted of first degree murder, and all five of them were subsequently sentenced to death. However, well before they had had time to exhaust the means of appeal available to them, capital punishment was abolished in California, and their sentences were consequently reduced to life imprisonment. They will, all of them, be entitled to apply for parole in 1978, though how long each of them will actually serve is a matter of conjecture. As far as one can tell, this is the one matter most people in California are chiefly concerned about.

Late in 1974 Vincent Bugliosi, the young deputy district attorney who led for the prosecution, published in collaboration with Curt Gentry a long and very detailed book about the murders entitled *Helter Skelter*.[50] One may note that he entitles the epilogue 'A Shared Madness' and (for example) writes of Susan Atkins when he first met her, 'She was crazy. I had no doubt about it.

Opposite: Charles Manson, whose appearance was remarkable for its chameleon quality

Opposite above: Sharon Tate's body being removed from her house (below) Inset: Sharon Tate with her husband Roman Polansky

Probably not legally insane, but crazy none the less.' Yet though Mr Bugliosi holds that 'the primary duty of a lawyer in a public prosecution is not to convict, but to see that justice is done', he was avowedly determined not only to secure convictions, but to win a recommendation from the jury for death in each case.

One may consider the question of Manson's sanity in the light of what the prosecution alleged was his motive for ordering the killings. Aaron Stovitz, who was associated with Bugliosi, strongly recommended something simple enough for a jury to be relied on to understand: for instance, the possibility that Manson was hoping to raise the $625 needed to bail out Mary Brunner, mother of one of his several offspring, who had been arrested the night before the Tate murders for stealing a credit card. But Bugliosi preferred what he was convinced was the real motive: 'to instil fear into the pigs' and bring on 'Helter Skelter', or a war between blacks and whites which would end in the total extermination of the whites. Bugliosi realized that a jury would dismiss this motive as too fantastic for belief unless he could find what he calls 'the missing link'—the thing that Manson had personally to gain from Helter Skelter. He did, in fact, discover this when he learned of the 'bottomless pit' in the desert, where Manson intended to take refuge with his followers. For Manson was certain that the time would come when the black man would realize that he couldn't handle things without being told by the white man what to do, and he would be forced to ask Charlie for help. The Family, by then multiplied to 144,000 (as prophesied in the Book of Revelations), would emerge from the bottomless pit a pure white master race, and Charlie would rule the world. Thus the motive, as Bugliosi saw it, was clear: murder done out of lust for power and gain. 'In his sick, twisted, disordered mind, Charles Manson believed that he would be the ultimate beneficiary of the black-white war and the murders which triggered it.'

If that was, indeed, his motive—and Bugliosi had plenty of evidence to prove that it was—it must surely follow that Manson was a lunatic, except according to the strictest interpretation of the legal or M'Naghten test under which no one is held to be insane who knows that what he is doing the law considers wrong.

Following pages: Some of those connected with the Manson investigation; by no means all were involved in criminal activity, and some gave evidence for the prosecution

Even more importantly, it is certain that the federal penal authorities bear a large measure of responsibility for the fact that the murders took place at all. 'God, Vince,' a reporter said to Bugliosi outside the courtroom, 'did it ever occur to you that if Barrett had revoked

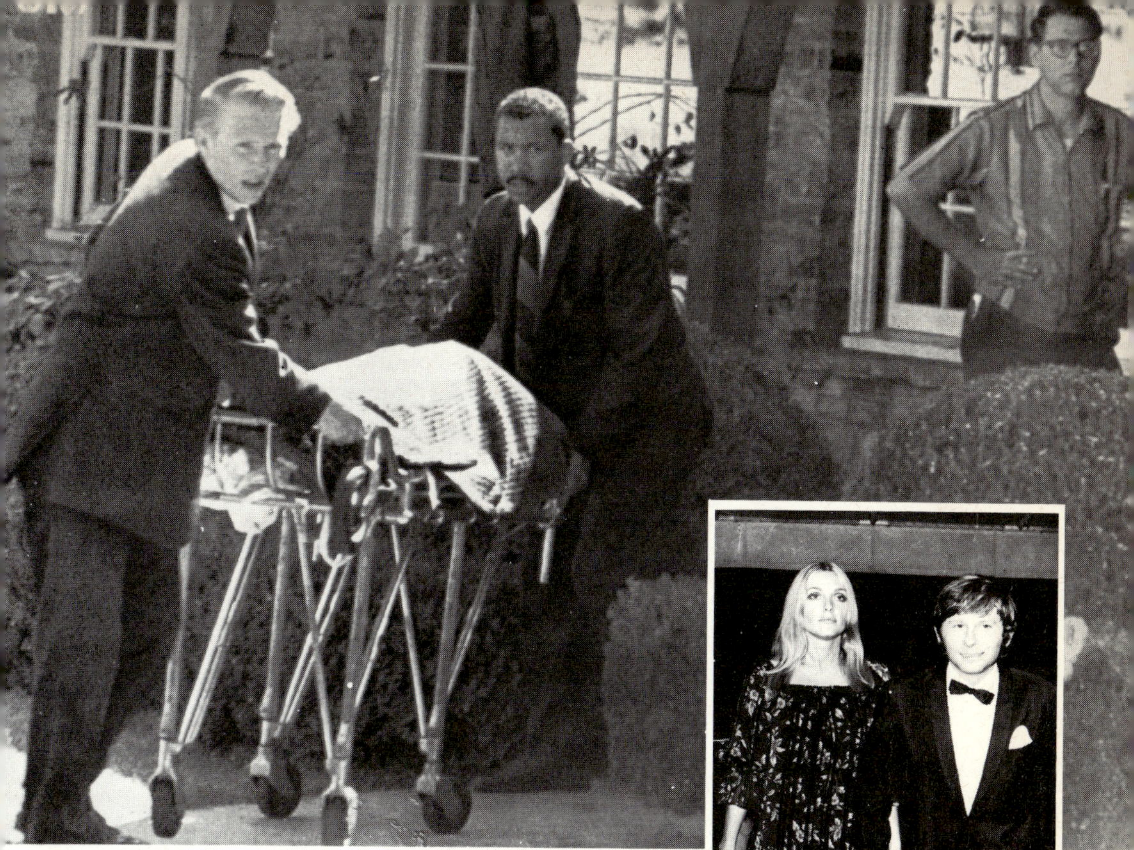

VANCE, Bill
AKA: HAMIC, David Lee
SCHWARM, Duane
PHOTO 5780
PHOTO 5755
PHOTO 5758
VAN HOUTEN, Leslie
AKA: SANKSTON, Leslie Mary
ATKINS, Susan Denise
AKA: GLUTZ, Sadie Mae
PHOTO 5807
PHOTO 5806
Stephanie Jean
HANUM, David Brian
CRAVEN, Larry Eugene
AKA: "Little Larry" Jones

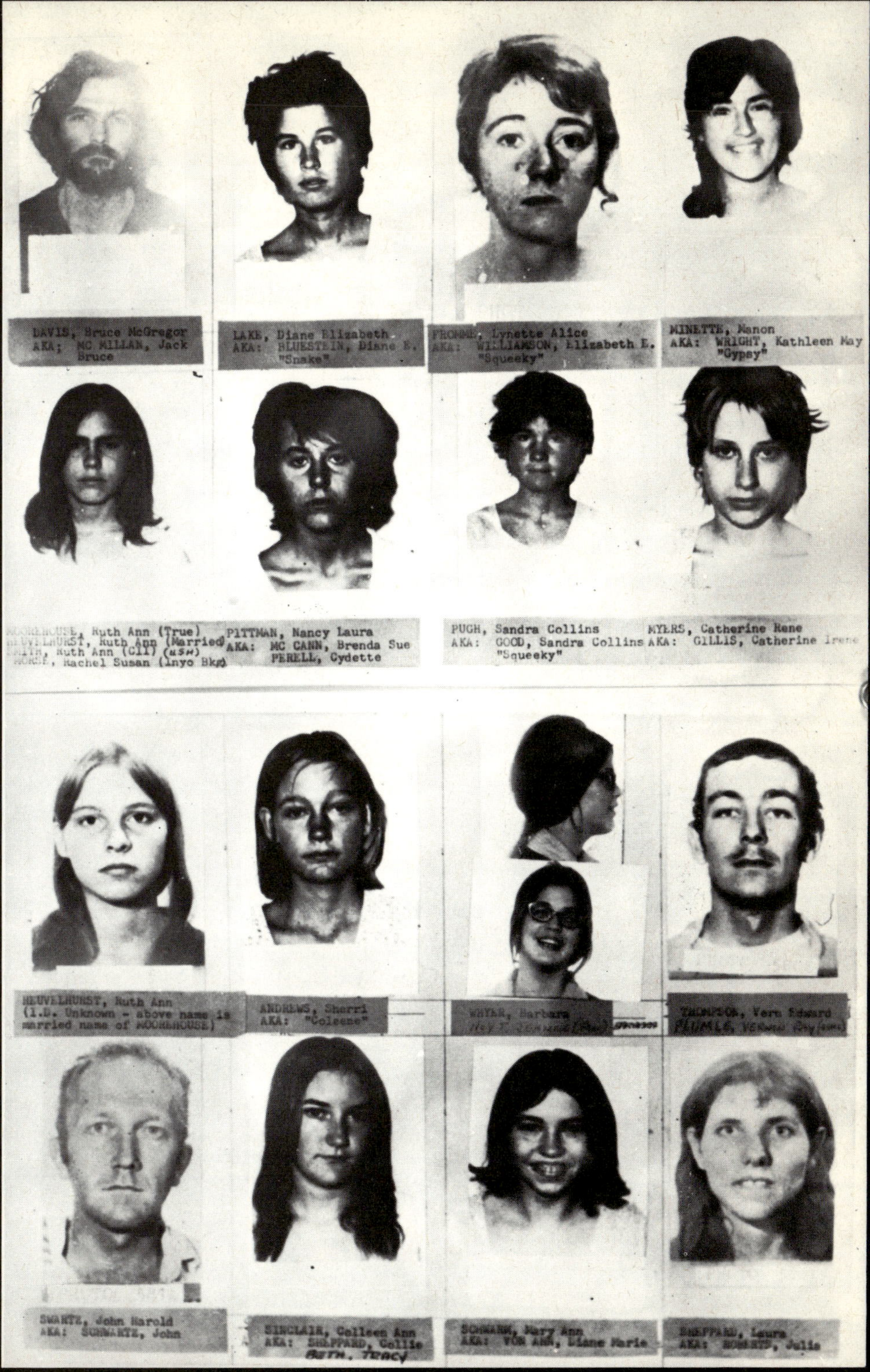
DAVIS, Bruce McGregor
AKA; MC MILLAN, Jack Bruce
LAKE, Diane Elizabeth
AKA: BLUESTEIN, Diane E.
"Snake"
FROMME, Lynette Alice
AKA: WILLIAMSON, Elizabeth E.
"Squeeky"
MINETTE, Manon
AKA: WRIGHT, Kathleen May
"Gypsy"
MOORHOUSE, Ruth Ann (True)
HEUVELHURST, Ruth Ann (Married)
SMITH, Ruth Ann (CII) (USM)
MORSE, Rachel Susan (Inyo Bkg)
PITTMAN, Nancy Laura
AKA: MC CANN, Brenda Sue
PERELL, Cydette
PUGH, Sandra Collins
AKA: GOOD, Sandra Collins
"Squeeky"
MYERS, Catherine Rene
AKA: GILLIS, Catherine Irene
HEUVELHURST, Ruth Ann
(I.D. Unknown - above name is married name of MOORHOUSE)
ANDREWS, Sherri
AKA: "Coleene"
WHYAR, Barbara
THOMPSON, Vern Edward
PLUMLE, Vernon
SWARTZ, John Harold
AKA: SCHWARTZ, John
SINCLAIR, Colleen Ann
AKA: SHEPPARD, Collie
RUTH, TRACY
SCHRAM, Mary Ann
AKA: VON ANN, Diane Marie
SHEPPARD, Laura
AKA: ROBERTS, Julie

Manson's parole in, say, April, 1969, Sharon and the others would probably still be alive today?' The real point was much stronger than that. For while Samuel Barrett, Manson's parole officer, was given plenty of cause to revoke Manson's parole before the murders, Manson himself had not wanted this parole when it was granted him in 1967. In fact, he pleaded with the authorities to let him stay in prison, saying that prison had become his home and that he did not think he could adjust to the outside world. His request was refused, despite the fact that the only chance of success in the free community that he had—and this was no more than a chance—was to be placed in the charge of some skilled and understanding person who could devote his whole time to him. As it was, he was dealt with like every other parolee: made answerable to a man who had 150 other people either on parole or probation to look after. And Manson made it clear in a talk with Bugliosi, which took place in June 1971, after the case was over, that he was glad to be back in prison, again calling it his 'home'.

Psychiatry, which has been called the science of prediction, should also acknowledge some blame. Manson was the illegitimate son of a 16-year-old girl. She lived with numerous men, and married one of them who gave Manson his name. In 1939, when he was 5, his mother was sentenced to five years for armed robbery, and Manson was cared for by an uncle and aunt who were deeply religious. What influence they had on him, if any, is not known; but his mother reclaimed him after she was paroled in 1942, and he went to share her drunken and promiscuous existence until she wearied of him. After a brief time in care at a school in Indiana from which he absconded, Manson's career of crime began. It took him through several states, landed him in various institutions, educational at the start but later punitive, and included burglary, armed robbery, fraud, forgery, sodomy and pimping, with a high proportion of federal as opposed to state offences, for which penalties are likely to be far more severe.

During his periods of liberty, he was twice married. He had a son by his first wife Rosalie. The son was born while he was once more in jail. Though he had beaten Rosalie at times, he called her 'the best wife a guy could want'.[51] She subsequently went to live with another man, and divorced him. His second wife Leona was a known prostitute for whom he pimped. He had been granted probation in 1959 instead of a ten-year sentence, on Leona's plea that she was pregnant by him, which was a lie, and that they were deeply in love. In February of the next year, Manson introduced himself to one Jo Anne Samuels as the president of '3-Star Enterprises, Nite Club and TV Enterprises'. He persuaded this girl to invest all her savings in the company, which didn't exist, drugged and raped her room-mate, and got Jo Anne herself pregnant. On 23 June 1960 he was sent to serve out his ten-year sentence, the judge observing that 'If there ever was a man who demonstrated himself completely unfit for probation, he is it'.[52] After spending a year in the Los Angeles County Jail, he arrived at the United States Penitentiary at McNeil Island, Washington, in July 1961.

It is understandable that Manson should have come to consider prison his 'home' and have dreaded leaving it, for he did comparatively well at the McNeil Island penitentiary, and found in it a security which he had learned did not exist for him in the outside world. He was, it is true, chronically unstable in his interests, and those interests were largely of an outré or trendy kind. For example, he studied scientology under the guidance of a fellow-convict, and, according to his own claim, ultimately attained the highest level of 'beta clear'. Again, in 1964, when the Beatles and Beatlemania came to the United States, Manson learned to play the steel guitar. The last report on him before his release was made in August 1966, and said that 'he has come to worship his guitar and music', but also said that he had 'no plans for release as he says he has nowhere to go'.[53]

Since the age of 12 Manson had spent seventeen years in institutions, and his remaining three years in the free world during the same period had been constantly criminal. Two psychiatrists had seen him. The first of them, Dr Block, met him when he was 17, and after treating him with individual psychotherapy over a period of three months plainly failed to recognize the extreme potential dangerousness in him. For in the belief that he 'needed to be trusted' he recommended his transfer from the National Training School for Boys in Washington, D.C., to the minimum security Natural Bridge Honor Camp, where in less than three months he was found guilty of an offence which got him sent to the Federal Reformatory at Petersburg, Virginia. He held a razor blade against another boy's throat while committing an act of sodomy on him.

The other psychiatrist to see Manson was Dr Edwin McNiel, who interviewed him on two occasions in response to a judge's request. The first was in 1955 when he appears merely to have listened to what Manson had to say for and about himself, and then to have made a routine sort of report which one would suppose might have come from anybody else: 'It is evident that he has an unstable personality and that his environmental influences throughout most of his life have not been good . . . In my opinion this boy is a poor risk for probation; on the other hand, he has spent nine years in institutions with apparently little benefit except to take him out of circulation. With the incentive of a wife and probably fatherhood, it is possible that he might be able to straighten himself out. I would, therefore, respectfully recommend to the court that probation be considered in this case under careful supervision.'

The second occasion on which Dr McNiel saw Manson was before Leona made her plea, and this time his recommendation was against the probation order which the judge none the less made. But Dr McNiel still did no more than interview Manson. He had as little success as Dr Block had had in predicting the magnitude of the menace in him; nor did he suggest that the proper place for a man of his kind was not a prison, where he could merely be kept out of circulation for a few years, but a secure hospital where he could be retained indefinitely and to which he would probably have been perfectly willing to go.

The power that Manson exhibited after his release on parole—a power of which there had been no evidence in his previous criminal career—to attract and dominate a 'family' of both sexes is for the moment inexplicable, except in psychic terms. Bugliosi said of the other defendants, 'True, Watson, Atkins, Krenkwinkel, and Van Houten committed these murders because Charles Manson told them to, but they would never have committed these murders in a million years if they did not already have murder in their guts, in their system. Manson merely told them to do what they were already capable of doing.' Can one really believe so simple an explanation? Not, surely, when one considers that Robert Beausoleil, 22, Mary Brunner, 23, Steve Grogan, 17, and Bruce Davis, 26, who all belonged to the Manson Family, were proven murderers, and at least six others were known either to have done murder or been willing to do it. They were all drop-outs. They may all have been 'crazy', though 'not legally insane'. But did Manson really collect so many in so short a time with 'murder in their guts, in their system'?

I was present by chance on one day only of the Sharon

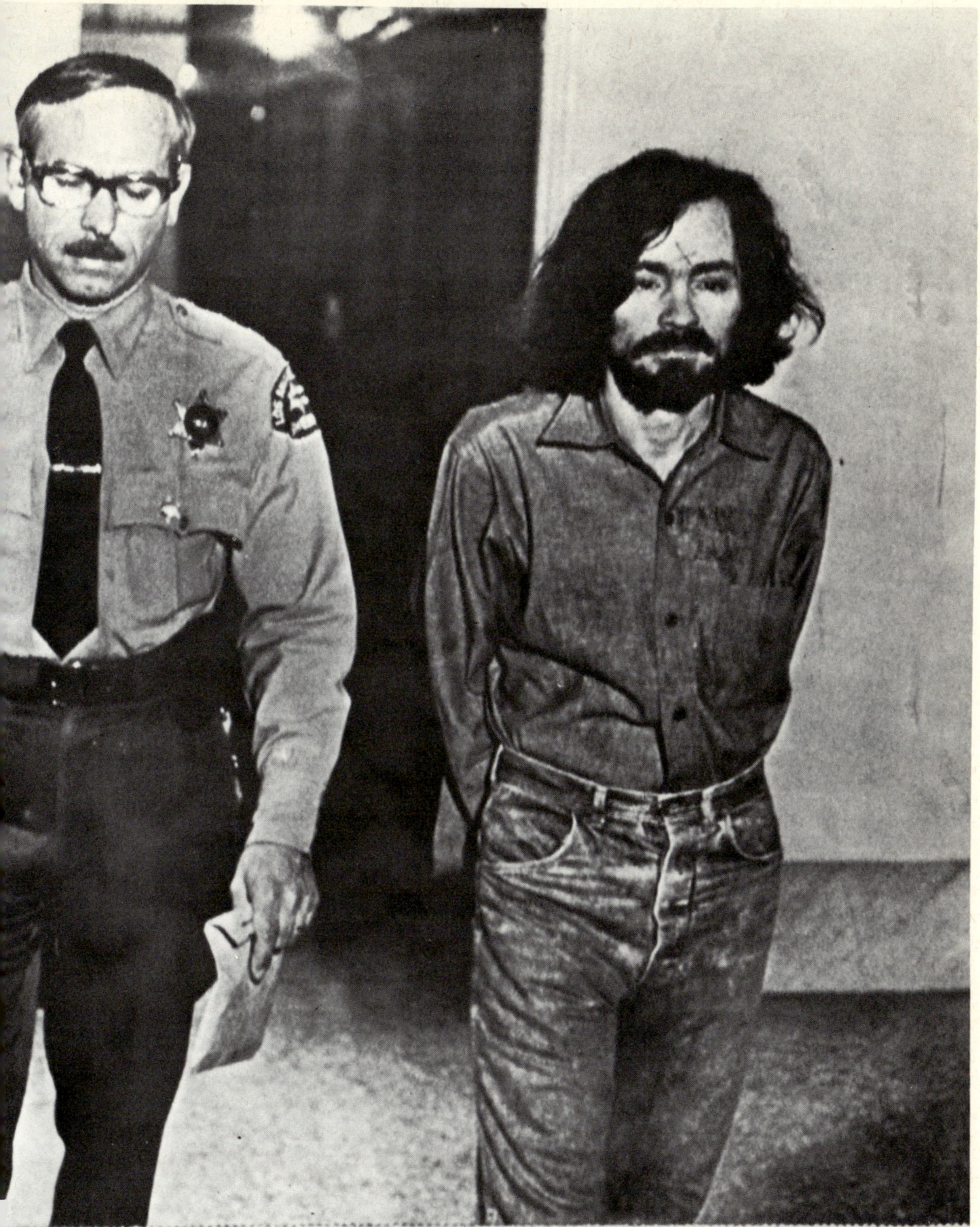

(LA1) LOS ANGELES, Aug. 11--MANSON STALKS INTO COURT--Charles M. Manson, a scratched cross on his forehead still visible, is led to court today by a deputy sheriff for another session of his trial on murder charges resulting from the deaths of actress Sharon Tate and six others. Manson looked neither to left or right as he marched into the courtroom. (AP Wirephoto)(rhs31100pl) 1970

MANSON, 3 GUILTY

"I think the jury's guilty," said Charles Manson as he was led from court. (AP)

Killed Sharon Tate and six others

LOS ANGELES (UPI) — Charles Manson and three young women he lured into his nomadic cult were convicted of first-degree murder Monday in the murders of actress Sharon Tate and six others.

A predominantly middle-aged jury returned a verdict finding the self-styled "Jesus Christ" guilty of sending members of his cult out to stab and shoot to death five persons at the Tate home and two others at the residence of wealthy supermarket owner Leno LaBianca.

The women — Susan Atkins, 22, Patricia Krenwinkel, 23, and Leslie Van Houten, 21 — also were convicted of first-degree murder. Miss Van Houten, a former high school beauty queen, was charged only with the LaBianca slayings.

Fate up to jury

The same jury will decide whether the 36-year-old Manson and the three girls will get life imprisonment or death in the gas chamber. The prosecutor said he will ask for death.

"You'll never live to see that day," Manson snarled to Judge Charles J. Older as he was led from a courtroom swarming with armed deputies.

The girls giggled after the verdicts were read and one said: "Oh doesn't the jury look sad!"

The four were convicted largely on the eyewitness testimony of Linda Kasabian, 20, who joined the weird commune only a month before the August, 1969, slayings and who was given immunity from prosecution in exchange for turning informer. She is living with her mother and two children in New Hampshire.

Weigh Penalties Thursday

The penalty phase of the trial will begin Thursday. Deputy Dist. Atty. Vincent Bugliosi said he expected to call about 50 witnesses in support of the state demand that all four go to the gas chamber at San Quentin.

Manson heard the verdicts in silence but then began calling to the judge: "Hey, Pops. Look at me, Pops."

"We weren't allowed to put on a defense, old man," he said. "I think the jury's guilty."

The three young women, dressed in blue

Turn to Page 8

SHARON TATE

LEFT: Found guilty with Manson in the Tate-LaBianca slayings, (l. to r.) Patricia Krenwinkel, Susan Atkins and Leslie Van Houten smile as they are escorted from courtroom. (UPI)

Senate group calls Rogers on Cambodia

Chicago Sun-Times, 26 January 1971

Tate trial, which lasted more than six months. I had been warned that it would be an exceptionally dull day confined to legal arguments. The prosecution had just concluded its case, and it had at once appeared that there was a dispute between the defendants and their counsel. The three girls had wished to testify to their own guilt in order to exculpate Manson. Rather than permit them to do this the defence had decided to rest its case. The session had ended in an unresolved deadlock. It was presumed that Manson had ordered the girls to take the blame for him, and that they were determined to obey him.

Even if this was so, Manson must obviously have changed his mind by the next day, because as soon as

the proceedings began in the half-empty courtroom (comparatively few people, including reporters, were interested in legal arguments as opposed to blood) he took everyone by surprise with an offer to testify himself. The judge accepted this offer—I suspect gratefully, for it got him out of a very tricky situation—with the proviso that Manson should testify in the first place in the jury's absence in order that the admissibility of his testimony might be tested, and under these circumstances he was allowed to make a statement rather than be questioned by his counsel.

The three women convicted with Charles Manson of murder. Left to right: Leslie Van Houten, Patricia Krenkwinkel and Susan Atkins. Leslie Van Houten was subsequently granted a new trial

Manson spoke for more than an hour. It was a rambling, disorganized, largely irrelevant, and, I suppose, essentially mad speech, but utterly compelling; and I know that I, and I imagine everyone else who heard it, came away with the conviction that there must be some extraordinary power in Manson. 'I never growed up to read and write too good', he said near the beginning, which was the simple truth, but I felt he was making grammatical errors of this sort purposely to win our sympathy. Later, he lambasted us: 'If I could, I would jerk this microphone off and beat your brains out with it, because that is what you deserve, that is what you deserve.' At one point, he pictured himself as a sort of Peter Pan playing with his children a make-believe game of pirates and Indians in the woods; at another he betrayed bitterness about being forced to accept his parole: 'It's all your fear. You look for something to project it on, and you pick on a little old scroungy nobody that eats out of a garbage can, and that nobody wants, that was kicked out of the penitentiary, and that has been dragged out of every hellhole you can think of, and you drag him into a courtroom.' But he also revealed a flash of humour after the judge had asked him to stick to the issues. 'Mr Bugliosi is a hard-driving prosecutor, polished education, a master of words, semantics. He is a genius. He has got everything a lawyer would want to have except one thing—a case.'

Manson admitted that he might have implied that he was, possibly, Jesus Christ, but said that he himself hadn't yet decided what or who he was. 'You can do anything you want with me, but you cannot touch me, because I am only my love . . . If you put me in the penitentiary, that means nothing because you kicked me out of the last one. I didn't ask to get released. I liked it in there because I like myself.'

At the same time, though he took a while to get round to it, Manson denied his own guilt clearly and unequivocally. After saying that 'these children', by which he meant the three female defendants, would have to explain whatever they had done, he told us, 'I have killed no one and I have ordered no one to be killed.' That part of his speech at least was relevant, and would have been admissible had he chosen to repeat it in front of a jury.

But, amazingly, he did not so choose. He made his denial before the court officials and the few spectators who could not in any way influence the verdict. And when the judge asked him whether he wished to testify in the presence of the jury, Manson replied, 'I have already relieved all the pressure I had.'

On his way back from the stand to his seat (there is

no dock in a Californian court) I saw Manson speak hurriedly to the girls, and I guessed at the time that he was 'unprogramming' them, though I could not hear what he said. However, Bugliosi reports in his book: 'As Manson left the stand and passed the counsel table, I overheard him tell the three girls: "You don't have to testify now." The big question: what did he mean by "now"? I strongly suspected that Manson hadn't given up but was only biding his time.'

But though Bugliosi does not admit as much, his 'strong suspicion' was never fulfilled. And it is a question whether it was, in fact, Manson's idea originally that the girls should testify as they had planned, or whether he deliberately took the stand himself, without hope of doing himself any good thereby, to keep them off it.

It is not enough to call Manson insane, and leave it at that, though it might have been a lot fairer than what has been done to him. One wants to know the source of these strange powers, which evidently didn't exist before he was forced out of the federal penitentiary at McNeil Island. He was a little man—only five feet two. Boys murdered for him as well as girls, and though most of the girls claimed to be desperately in love with him, not all of them did. Leslie Van Houten, for instance, told the psychiatrist who examined her that 'Charles was short. That is something that always turned me off.'[55]

According to Bugliosi, Manson alone among the killers 'merits special handling', though by 'special' he evidently means particularly tough. For a while he was transferred to a maximum security 'adjustment centre' at Folsom Prison. The Warden of San Quentin said before his transfer: 'It would be dangerous to put a guy like Manson into the main population, because in the eyes of other inmates he didn't commit first-class crimes. He was convicted of killing a pregnant woman, and that sort of thing doesn't allow him to rank very high in the social structure. It's like being a child molester. Guys like that are going to do time hard wherever they are.'[56]

At Folsom Prison Manson lost all the inmate privileges that would normally be allowed him; no psychiatrist or anyone else who might be interested in his case went near him. He has since then been re-transferred to San Quentin, and was there when his chief disciple 'Squeaky' Fromme made a completely bungled effort to assassinate President Ford in 1975. But he is still presumably doing his 'time hard'; and even assuming that that is the kind of 'special attention' which he merits, it is not the kind from which society can hope to derive any benefit.

PART 4 ROBBERY

1/The Mayfair Boys

Robbery tends to be regarded as a crime committed by professionals or experts; and the publicity it receives usually corresponds, like the punishment it provokes, with the size of the haul. This is why the train robbery of 1963 may fairly be called the robbery of the century so far.

Opposite above: Three of the four Mayfair Boys. Left to right: Robert Harley, John Christopher Lonsdale, and David Wilmer

Below: Crowds queueing to get into the public gallery of the Old Bailey for the Mayfair trial, 1938

But there was an earlier case in Britain—the jewel theft of 1937—which caused nearly as big a sensation, though it was not the work of professional criminals at all, nor was it concerned with an especially vast amount of loot. It might ordinarily have passed without much more than fleeting notice, and in fact in America it was pretty well ignored.

How much interest a similar happening would arouse in the Britain of today would test the strength of the British social revolution. For the jewel theft was extraordinary only because of the identity of its participants. They were dubbed the Mayfair Boys; they spent most of their time in nightclubs and at bottle parties; and all four of them were products of famous English public schools. Robert Harley, 26, had been at Wellington; David Wilmer, 24, at Oundle; John Christopher Mainwaring Lonsdale, 24, at Radley; and Peter Martin Jenkins, 21, at Harrow.

There is little or no doubt about what they actually did. At 1.15 p.m. on 20 December 1937 Jenkins engaged a suite of rooms at the Hyde Park Hotel in London, with two outside doors, one leading to the drawing room, the other to the bedroom. He used the name of E. L. Hambro of Wimborne Court, Dorset, said that his luggage would be arriving later, and ordered a bottle of whisky and some glasses to be sent up. He then telephoned Cartiers, and spoke to a director, Mr Etienne Bellenger, saying he would like him to bring round a selection of rings since he wished to choose one for a lady with very expensive tastes. Mr Bellenger readily agreed to come, for he already knew Mr Hambro of Wimborne Court by reputation. The appointment was fixed for three-thirty that afternoon.

Before Bellenger arrived, Lonsdale had come, presumably to see how things were going, and had left again. Bellenger was taken up in the lift, having been kept waiting for a while in the lobby, and he encountered David Wilmer who was inquiring for the same numbered entrance to the drawing room, though actually Wilmer had been there before. Bellenger was given to understand that Wilmer was Jenkins's secretary, and twice while he was showing Jenkins the rings he had brought for his consideration Wilmer left them to go into the bedroom.

Wilmer was back again after Jenkins had said that he wished to see a ring under electric light, and Bellenger was standing, the ring in his hand, with his back to the half-open bedroom door. At that moment Wilmer gave some sort of sign, and Bellenger was aware of a sudden crack on the head. He turned to face Harley. The lower part of Harley's face was covered by a handkerchief, he was wearing tinted glasses, and was wielding what looked like a black mallet. Bellenger tried to push the glasses into Harley's eyes, but his strength was ebbing under a rain of blows. Then Wilmer pushed him to the ground and said 'Come on! Finish it!' Harley hit him several times more until he lay still. He was not unconscious, but he thought he was going to be killed, and he almost certainly would have died if he hadn't happened to be possessed of an unusually thick skull.

Jenkins had simply watched the assault without taking any part in it, and may have hurried away (there is some confusion in the evidence here) a minute or two ahead of the other two. It is certain that between them they grabbed all the jewels, except for the £3,000 ring which Bellenger was carrying when he was attacked and which had rolled under a settee. It is also certain that they left Bellenger with his head lying in a pool of blood, and neither knew nor apparently cared whether he was alive or dead. In fact, about a quarter of an hour after their departure Bellenger managed to attract the attention of a chambermaid. A doctor was called for, and he was rushed to hospital. It was more than a month before he was well enough to give evidence in court.

Later in the evening of the robbery Lonsdale met his three confederates at the Nineteenth Club in Cork Street. The rings were all entrusted to Harley, who at about 4 a.m. next morning went to his brother's house in Kensington and hid the rings behind some waste pipes. Meanwhile Lonsdale and Jenkins got into Wilmer's car, and Wilmer drove them to Oxford, where they arrived in the early hours of the morning. They put up at the Clarendon Hotel, both of them registering under false names and Jenkins again demanding a suite. Wilmer drove on to stay with a titled aunt in Gloucestershire.

Within twenty-four hours of the theft, the rings had been recovered and all four of the culprits were under arrest. The police had happened on plenty of evidence in the Hyde Park Hotel suite; it included a whisky bottle and a tumbler with what turned out to be Jenkins's fingerprints on them, another tumbler with what turned out to be Wilmer's fingerprints on it, a third tumbler with the remains of whisky in it but without any fingerprints, a pair of gloves which were found to be an 'excellent fit' for Harley, a packet of Chesterfield cigarettes and Chesterfield cigarette ends, the brand which, it turned out, Harley habitually smoked. All this evidence (and more) would not have been enough to enable the police to move so quickly, if the suspicions of the night porter at the Oxford Clarendon Hotel had not been aroused by the behaviour of Jenkins and Lonsdale, particularly by Jenkins's demand for a suite. For these young men, though playboys and not particularly reputable, had no record as jewel thieves. Indeed, Harley hadn't a criminal record of any kind, and the other three had been guilty of only very minor offences.

The question of why they committed so ugly an offence remains something of a mystery. Peter Jenkins in a book published fifteen years later, 1952, while describing the incident as an 'unspeakable outrage', argues that the young men were all so besotted with drink that they had little or no idea of what they were doing.[57] They were not, he says, more than usually hard up, and would have been prepared to surrender the jewels as soon as they came to their senses. He denies emphatically that violence was ever contemplated, and maintains that he was horrified when it occurred.

If this account of the affair deals too generously with Jenkins himself, it is far more generous to Harley, whom it describes (without directly naming him) as 'the masked man, who still stood waving his cosh about in a drunken frenzy for several seconds before he realized that his unfortunate victim had fallen'. It does not mention the fact, which one would suppose Jenkins might still have felt extremely bitter about, that in two separate statements to the police Harley attempted to shift all the blame from himself on to his confederates. Harley swore in the witness box that he had taken the rings only with a view to collecting on the insurance. He denied that he had ever gone nearer to the suite than the lobby of the hotel, where he met Wilmer. He also said that the plan of attacking Bellenger had been suggested to him by Jenkins and Wilmer, but that he had had nothing to do with it.

Jenkins's treatment of Harley in his book may, under the circumstances, seem extraordinarily gallant and forgiving. But allowing for this, it is still hard to accept that there was no more to the 'unspeakable outrage' than a sort of youthful, drunken prank which went wrong.

Jenkins says that the scheme was cooked up under the influence of the whisky bottle by four young men, all of whom were 'reluctant to do anything dishonest', but none of whom dared say so for fear of earning the contempt of his fellows; and he says that it was carried out by three of the young men, one of whom was positively mad with drink.

Jenkins, however, refrains from admitting that he himself had a criminal record; he had been bound over for obtaining credit by fraud, and had passed a number of worthless cheques. He is also guilty of at least one evident error of fact when he says that at the final police court hearing Inspector Burt vigorously opposed bail for all four defendants, largely on the grounds that they had arranged for an aeroplane in a private field to fly them out of the country. But this aeroplane story, which Jenkins says was 'a new one on them', though it was reported in the press after their conviction, was not referred to at all by Inspector Burt. What the Inspector did do was to inform Lonsdale's solicitor privately of his reason (which he did not disclose in public) for objecting to the continuance of bail for Lonsdale. This had been granted during the first week's remand, when bail had been refused the other three defendants. The reason must have been compelling, because the solicitor made no demur and Lonsdale was thereupon remanded in custody.

But when all this has been said, it would seem even more unlikely that the crime was what Lord Hewart (the Lord Chief Justice of England) apparently imagined it to be: a carefully considered conspiracy to steal valuable rings, with violence its inevitable concomitant. For clearly if the conspirators had had the wit and the will to cover their tracks, they could very easily have done so without any immediate need of an aeroplane to fly them out of the country. There was no reason, on the face of it, why they should ever have come under suspicion.

Nor was violence—or at least the degree of violence which was used—in the least necessary. Jenkins says that the original plan was for him simply to walk, with several rings in his hand, from the drawing room to the bedroom on the pretext of looking for his cheque book, and then make his getaway through the bedroom door before Bellenger had time to realize that anything was amiss. Granted this either proved impractical, or was never really intended, it would surely have been possible for Jenkins, Harley and Wilmer between them to overpower and gag Bellenger without doing him serious injury.

They could perfectly safely have taken their time afterwards both in removing the rings and in covering all traces of their presence in the suite. Instead, they hurried away, presumably panic-stricken, though Harley was allegedly giggling or laughing, having grabbed most of the loot, but leaving behind, quite needlessly, the evidence that convicted them.

In short, if they really were participants in a carefully planned conspiracy, their execution of it was conducted with quite incredible stupidity. Yet it was even alleged in one newspaper (though one does not know whether the Lord Chief Justice had private convictions of a similar sort) that a 'Mr Big', a continental figure who was still living in luxurious freedom, was the brains behind the enterprise. Some Mr Big, one is tempted to add, some brains!

Jenkins describes the actual trial as a social spectacle where opera glasses would not have seemed out of place, and in this he is certainly justified. Not only was the public gallery packed, with hundreds of disappointed people turned away, but there were reserved seats in the well of the courtroom for distinguished visitors such as the Countess of Oxford and Asquith, the Duke of Rutland, Viscountess Byng and Sir Seymour Hicks. Presumably nearly all these spectators, the fashionable ones occupying the reserved seats equally with the common throng in the public gallery, were there to watch the agony (or what they hoped would be the agony) of the four ex-public school boys in the dock. Undoubtedly, their interest was in what their punishment would be; they didn't have, couldn't have had, any serious doubts about their guilt. Nor, though important counsel were briefed for the defence, could they have been looking forward to an absorbing legal battle.

Eventually, Lonsdale was convicted of conspiracy to steal only; the others of robbery as well. In passing sentence, the Lord Chief Justice made a much quoted and applauded remark, which sounded profound enough but was in fact somewhat meaningless. 'If I believed that you really were educated men', he said, 'it would be necessary for me to be, on that account, more severe. Probably all that is meant is that somebody has spent money in providing you with certain conventional opportunities of education. The results are not impressive.'[58]

He gave Lonsdale eighteen months' hard labour, Jenkins, who had not been involved in the actual infliction of violence, three years' penal servitude, Wilmer five

TWO MAYFAIR PLAYBOY GANGSTERS GET CAT

Planned To Flee Country By Air After Hotel Attack On Bond-street Jeweller

'I CAN TAKE IT' BOAST

TWENTY strokes of the "cat" face one of the Mayfair playboys for his part in the £13,000 jew·; robbery at the Hyde Park Hotel.

Fifteen strokes face a second.

These were the full sentences on the four men—

Robert Paul Harley: Seven years' penal servitude and two years' hard labour (concurrently), and twenty strokes of the "cat," for conspiracy, robbery and violence.

David Wilmer: Five years' penal servitude and two years' hard labour (concurrently), and fifteen strokes of the "cat" for conspiracy, robbery and violence.

Peter Martin Jenkins: Three years' penal servitude and two years' hard labour (concurrently), for conspiracy, robbery and violence.

John Christopher Mainwaring Lonsdale: Eighteen months' hard labour for conspiracy.

Harley, who heard his sentence with a smile, lost his nerve when he reached his Old Bailey cell. "Seven years and twenty with the cat!" he groaned.

But by the time his brother was admitted he was grinning again. "Don't look so glum," he said. "It's pretty stiff, but I can take it."

Lord Hewart, the Lord Chief Justice, before sentencing the men, said the word "education" had been used.

"Somebody spent money in providing you with the conventional opportunities for education," said Lord Hewart. "The results are not impressive."

Lord Hewart described the attack on Mr. Bellenger as "an unspeakable outrage."

Wilmer, it is now revealed, made an attempt to leave the country by airplane immediately after the attack. He offered an ex-war pilot £50 for the trip.

Robert Paul Harley, who received yesterday the heaviest sentence of the four "Mayfair men," was known by many people prominent in the West End. In this picture he is at a night club party. A number of well-known people were there. At their request their faces have been painted out.

'I Am Not Sorry For Them'

—Attacked Jeweller

By LINDON LAING

WHEN Mr. Etienne Bellenger, the middle-aged jeweller who had his skull fractured in six places when he was lured to the Hyde Park Hotel and attacked, heard the sentences on the four Mayfair men, he said to me: "I am not sorry for them. Why should I be?"

Lonsdale, sleek and icy cool throughout the four-day trial, heard his sentence without a tremor, and marched from the dock like a soldier.

Jenkins came next. There was perspiration on his face. He was trembling.

Wilmer, blind in one eye, turned pale and almost cried—blinked to hide his tears—when he ·ard Lord Hewart say ". . . and fifteen strokes from the cat o' nine tails."

Harley, powerful, tall, his thick black moustache accentuating the pallor of his face, just turned away with a grin.

But in the cells below the Old Bailey he lost his nerve for a moment, and groaned, "Seven years and twenty with the cat!"

But by the time his brother was admitted to see him he was grinning again, and said "Don't look so glum. It's pretty stiff, but I can take it."

Two warders escorted each man from the dock in turn.

KEPT APART

Special precautions were taken to keep Harley away from both Wilmer and Jenkins who had been accused of lying—saying that Harley was the man who, disguised by dark glasses and a handkerchief over the lower part of his face, struck the blows that felled Mr. Bellenger—in order to save their own skins.

The doors of the court were locked while Lord Hewart summed

DENIES ENGAGEMENT TO PETER JENKINS

Sentence Of The Cat Means This:

HARLEY and Wilmer will not get the "cat" until they begin their penal servitude in Maidstone Jail.

They spent last night, with Jenkins and Lonsdale, in Wormwood Scrubs, the receiving prison for London area first offenders. The "cat" is not applied until prisoners have got over the shock of conviction.

It consists of a short, cloth-covered handle, to which are attached nine cords, each about one-eighth inch thick and thirty-three inches long. It is not knotted or reinforced with metal tags.

Harley and Wilmer will be specially examined by the prison doctors on their arrival in Maidstone. The doctors will determine the fitness of the prisoners to bear their punishment. Prisoners, in disputed cases, have the right to call a doctor of their own.

Final medical examinations are made on the day of punishment. Harley and Wilmer will be taken separately to the punishment shed.

The "cat" will be administered in the presence of the prison governor, medical officer and chief jailer. Harley and Wilmer's doctors will attend, if necessary.

The number of strokes are determined by the doctors and the prison governor. Few men in recent years have had more than three strokes at a time.

Punishment is repeated as soon as the prisoner is fit, usually after three weeks. At that rate Harley would not complete his sentence of twenty strokes for about five months.

News Summary

THE first deserted wife to seek a divorce under the new Matri-

DOCTOR TO PAY DANCER £1,000

WINIFRED GRACE WILSON, twenty-five-year-old dancer, was awarded £1,000 damages for breach of promise against twenty-eight-year-old Dr. Eric Redgewell Dansie in the King's Bench Division yesterday evening.

The crowd in court applaude[d] the jury's verdict and calle[d] "Hear, hear."

Afterwards Miss Wilson sai[d] "I can never forget Eric. I hav[e] hated this action all through. [I] really do love him."

(See Page Eleven)

Third Fire In Battleship

French Docks Inquir[y]

Daily Express Correspondent

ST. LAZAIRE, Friday.—Fire bro[ke] out last night aboard the 26,50[0] ton French battleship Strasbou[rg] nearing completion at St. Lazaire.

At least £7,000 damage was do[ne] and the completion of the Stra[s]bourg—due in two months—is like[ly] to be delayed.

The fire has started a searchi[ng] inquiry in the dockyard. It is t[he] third in the same vessel in tw[o] months.

Briton Leading In World Ice Title Bi[d]

BERLIN, Friday.—British figu[re] skating champion H. Graham Sha[rp] leads in the first of the competitio[ns] for the world championship, t[he] compulsory figures.

He is only 1.7 points in front [of] the holder, Felix Kaspar, of Aust[ria] (who beat Sharp for the Europe[an] title last month), but if he perfor[ms] up to his known capabilities in t[he] free skating he should win.—Reut[er]

The King And Quee[n]

Daily Express, 19 February 1938

years' penal servitude plus fifteen strokes of the cat, Harley seven years' penal servitude plus twenty strokes of the cat. It is impossible, in retrospect, to see how he could have justified these sentences. Granted he was right to believe that Harley and Wilmer deserved the cat in payment for their attack on Bellenger, why should he also have thought it proper to award them both longer prison terms than Jenkins, and Harley a longer prison term than Wilmer? They were all three of them equally guilty of the robbery. Moreover, if Bellenger had died they would all three of them have been convicted of murder and sentenced to death.

The cat-o'-nine-tails was an instrument of torture; and although it is now less than thirty years since it was outlawed, it seems as unlikely to be restored today as the stocks, the pillory, the ducking stool or the branding iron. In 1938, however, so short a while ago, there appeared to be vastly more people in favour of it than against it. When, for example, George Bernard Shaw wrote to the *Daily Telegraph* wittily questioning the propriety of the cat, he provoked a flood of angry correspondence, including a long letter from General Sir Neville Macready in praise of its deterrent effectiveness.

Meanwhile, the press had a heyday with its descriptions of precisely what the punishment was and how it was carried out. These were oddly contradictory. For instance, one could learn, according to which newspaper one read, that the cat was wielded by one warder, that it was wielded by two taking turns, that the punishment was traditionally inflicted in the early morning, that it was traditionally inflicted in the early afternoon, that a man after being flogged was always sent to the prison hospital, and that a man after being flogged was always sent back to work.

It would not have been surprising if the press had been correct in reporting on 1 March 1938 that Wilmer had collapsed after five strokes and Harley after six. But the press was evidently using its imagination again. For a few days later Sir Samuel Hoare, the Home Secretary, told a questioner in the House of Commons that the punishment had been carried out in full.

2/Joseph Redenbaugh, the Boston Brink's Robbery, the Great Train Robbery

A fundamental error, made alike by judges, penal authorities and psychiatrists, is to assume that all criminals can be neatly fitted into categories. Thus Joseph Redenbaugh had practised fraud, safe-breaking, robbery with violence, and finally murder for hire by the time he was 19, and thereafter he was locked up for forty-five years in Stillwater penitentiary, Minnesota. The judicial view of him was that he was irredeemably wicked, the penal view that he would be a dangerous escape risk until his spirit had been broken. The psychiatric view, if there had been one asked for, would almost certainly have been that he was an aggressive psychopath, whose psychopathy might eventually burn itself out.

But, in fact, Joseph Redenbaugh was from the very first determined to use Stillwater for self-education—as a preparation for the future—and his courage was indomitable. He was finally released at the age of 64, when most men are ready for retirement, and he has led an eminently constructive life ever since. He is still working today aged 77 at the time of writing (March 1976).

He knew at once, though he suffered from no remorse, that he would never again be a hired gun, but even after twenty years of incarceration he couldn't have sworn that he would renounce stealing. 'Oh, sure, I'm pretty well educated by this time', he told me once. 'But not as much as I am now. I hadn't thought as much about some things. Vestiges of the old life were there. I might have reverted to thieving and I might not.' But what would have tempted him? I wanted to know. 'Just the excitement probably. More the excitement and one thing and another like that than the actual money. Going out and doin' somethin' that was over and above what the ordinary guy could do.'

That may well be the motive of a good many of those who turn to robbery, including quite possibly the Mayfair Boys, though Joe's background was as lowly as theirs was privileged. He was born in extreme poverty, the son of a mother who sought solace in Christian Science without any understanding of it and a father who was an ambulant labourer and gambled away what little money he earned. As a child, Joe was regularly thrashed by both his parents for their different reasons.

But here again it doesn't follow, as the psychiatrists seem to imply, that the home background is the explanation or even part of the explanation of delinquency. 'Specs' O'Keefe, for instance, was the sixth of fifteen children of an assistant prison warden. Life for him was not luxurious, but neither was it deprived; and though it was to some extent disciplined, 'no whipping or anything like that' ever took place. Yet Specs O'Keefe made his career in crime, and was among those who in 1950 robbed Brink's, the armoured truck firm, in Boston, Massachusetts.

The Brink's case because it netted close to three million dollars took pride of place among robberies until it was eclipsed by England's great mail train robbery of 1963, which netted over two and a half million pounds. The men who robbed Brink's carried guns, but used them only to threaten, and one does not know whether they would have resorted to violence if they'd been challenged. No charges were brought against them until 1956, six years after the commission of their crime, and only then because Specs O'Keefe was persuaded to turn state's evidence against his confederates, one of whom, Adolph 'Jazz' Maffie, had spent the whole of O'Keefe's share of the loot, which he had undertaken to mind while O'Keefe was serving a prison term on another charge. Apart from O'Keefe himself and Stanley Albert Guscovia, who had died, it would seem that everyone who had anything to do with either the planning or the operation of the crime was convicted and received condign punishment.

This was not true of the Great Train Robbery, which was an even more complex operation and was just as well prepared. In fact, it had the qualities of a highly successful commando raid, with all the equipment necessary, such as walkie-talkies, transport, and camouflage in the form of balaclavas. Each man was assigned his especial task, one in which he was expert, and if he failed in it he was on his own; that is to say, there would be no coming to his aid at the risk of endangering the whole venture.

Exact timing was also essential, and foreknowledge that on the night chosen for the raid the train would be carrying a very substantial amount of money. The robbers, therefore, must have had informants within British Rail and the Post Office, but these people have

Opposite: Aerial view of the scene of the Great Train Robbery, August 1963

never been identified. It is known, moreover, that the gang actually involved in the robbery was bigger than the gang eventually convicted. But this crime, unlike the Brink's robbery, has proved to be a very rare instance of honour among thieves. Those who paid the penalty for what they did, and may still be paying it, might have benefited from playing 'squealer', but they have consistently refused the part either in relation to each other or anyone else.

If they had behaved as sensibly, or with as much discipline, after the operation as they did before and during it, probably not one of them would ever have been caught. The Royal Mail train, bound from Glasgow to Euston, came to an unscheduled halt at the lonely spot of Sears Crossing, near Linslade in Buckinghamshire, at 3.30 a.m. on 8 August. The signals had been tampered with. Someone uncoupled the high value package coach, which was the second from the engine, disconnecting it from the rest of the coaches, and the driver of the train was forced to drive his engine forward for half a mile. The high value package coach was then broken into, the few Post Office workers overpowered, and the job of removing the mail bags to the waiting transport was begun. In the end, all but eight of the mail bags were removed, seven being left in the van and one on the embankment. The total take was £2,631,684.

The gang did not carry guns, though they pretended to have them available in order to frighten the Post Office workers into submission. It has been claimed that they had agreed among themselves, or, rather, had been instructed by the chief organizers of the raid, under no circumstances to use violence. Nevertheless, one of their number coshed the train driver Jack Mills, who was putting up considerable resistance. Although Mills was still able to drive the train, he was so badly injured that he was never to recover fully.

Despite the elaborate planning of the robbery itself and its brilliant execution, the aftermath was notable for the absence of any plan and makes it unlikely that there can have been some mastermind behind the enterprise, as several writers have suggested. The thieves carried their loot in a convoy of trucks to a nearby hide-out, Leatherslade Farm, and there the share-out took place. Most of the men behaved with extraordinary carelessness, considering they were professional thieves who must have realized that their hide-out would sooner or later be found and minutely examined by the police. They left their fingerprints behind.

CITY PRICES

TIO PEPE THE SHERRY OF SPAIN

Evening Standard

WEST END FINAL

CINZANO BIANCO

FRIDAY, AUGUST 9, 1963

The soaring total of the stolen notes would tower above the Vickers skyscraper

£2,525,100! AND IT'S STILL GOING UP

Rewards: £260,000 —and they're breaking all records too

Evening Standard Reporter

UP, UP, UP. Losses by banks alone in yesterday's great train robbery soared this afternoon to £2,525,000. And the rewards rose to a record total of £260,000.

The giant cash haul by the thieves was made up like this:

National Provincial [illegible]
Midland [illegible]
Barclays [illegible]
National Commercial Bank of Scotland [illegible]
British Linen [illegible]
Westminster [illegible]
Bank of Scotland [illegible]
Royal Bank of Scotland [illegible]
Total £2,525,100

Lloyds Bank says their loss is "negligible."

'Biggest-ever'

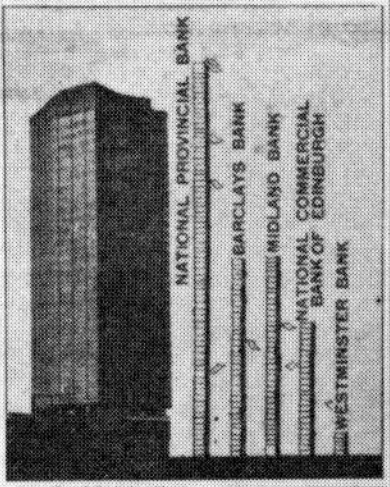

INSIDE NEWS

THE KENNEDY BABY DIES

PAGE ELEVEN

Mac says 'I do not cling to office'

PAGE TWELVE

Stratford: Mr Maude looks to Lord Avon

PAGE TWELVE

Edward Martell joins the Bristol battle

PAGE TWELVE

Stephen Ward inquest

PAGE TEN

Amusements Guide

PAGE NINE

WEATHER—rather cool—See Page 10

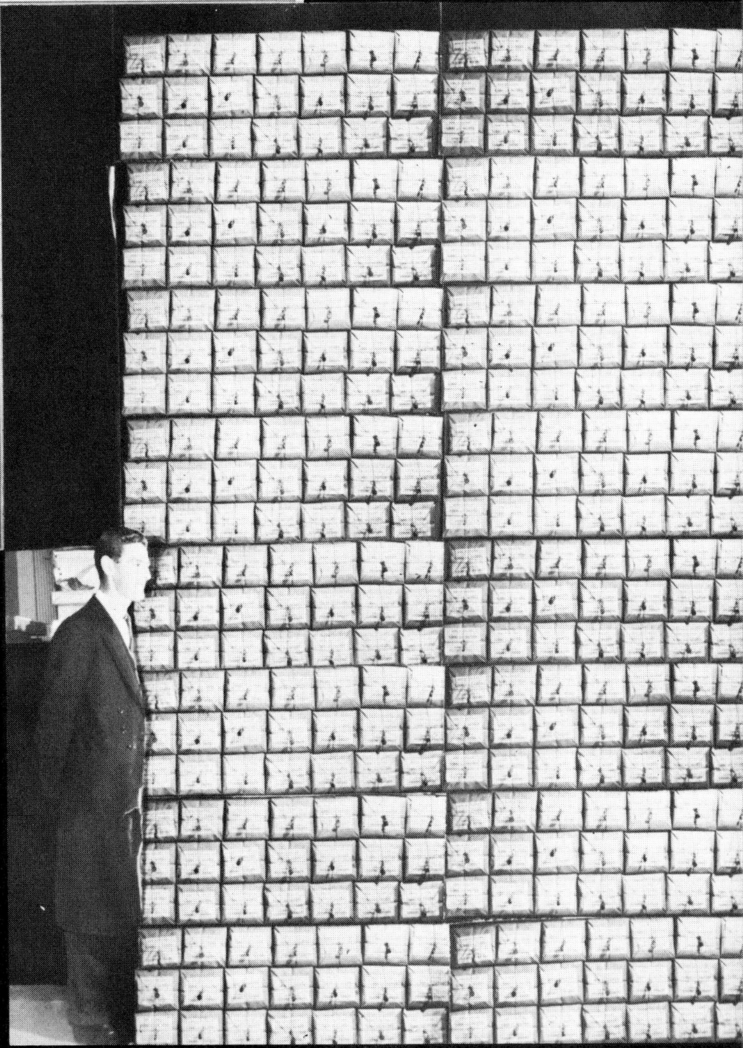

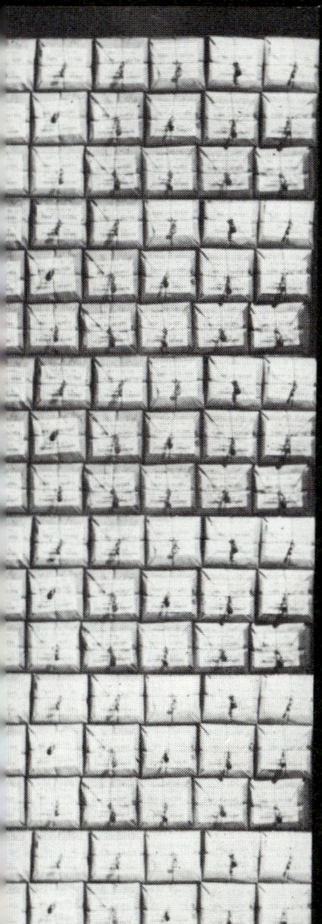

On 24 March 1964, after a trial that had lasted more than two months, nine men were convicted of actual participation in the robbery, and three others of assisting the robbers in one way or another. Of the nine, John Cordrey, who pleaded guilty and enabled the police to recover a large proportion of his share of the money after he had indulged in an immediate and wild spending spree, got twenty years (subsequently reduced to fourteen on appeal). William Gerald Boal, who was shown mercy partly on account of his age (he was 50) and partly because the judge did not believe him to be an originator of the conspiracy, got twenty-four years. The rest—Charles Wilson, Ronald Biggs, Thomas Wisbey, Robert Welch, James Hussey, Roy James, and Douglas Goody—got thirty years each. In some quarters these sentences were much criticized because of their severity. In others they were explained on the grounds of the violence done to the train driver. But it is safe to say that if one member of a gang seriously injured an old woman in pursuit of a robbery of, say, £1, the gang would not be nearly so harshly treated as these men were. In other words, it was the size of the haul that really dictated the length of the sentences. As the judge remarked, 'When grave crime is committed it calls for grave punishment, not for the purpose of mere retribution but so that others similarly tempted shall be brought to the sharp realization that crime does not pay and that crime is most certainly not worth the most alluring candle.'[59] What the judge meant by grave crime was in this instance crime against property, not against the person.

At the moment the judge spoke his sentencing speech, three other men whose fingerprints had been found at Leatherslade Farm were still on the loose. One of them, Bruce Reynolds, was undoubtedly a leader of the conspiracy, but after his arrest some five years later in November 1968 he came before a different judge and received a slightly more lenient sentence. 'Buster' Edwards, who surrendered in September 1966, claimed that he had visited the farm only after the robbery had been committed in order to 'clean up'—which, if he was telling the truth, he can't have done very well. Anyway, he was sentenced to a mere fifteen years and was paroled after serving nine of them. Most of the others have been paroled after serving twelve years, which is presumably considerably less time than the judge intended, but is still two years in excess of what was once admitted to be the maximum time that an average man could stand without suffering severe mental and physical deterioration.

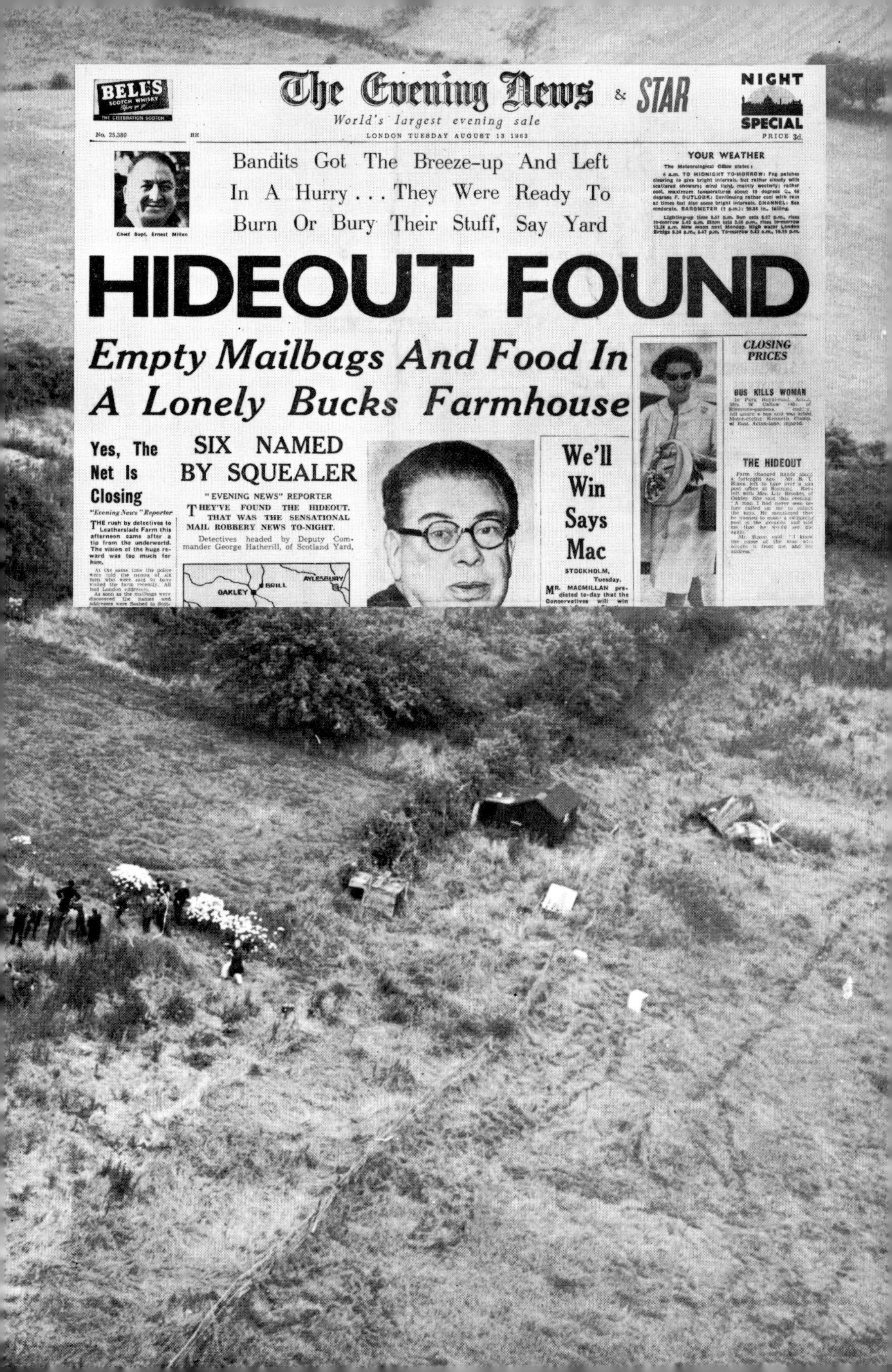

BELL'S SCOTCH WHISKY
THE CELEBRATION SCOTCH

The Evening News & STAR

World's largest evening sale

NIGHT SPECIAL

No. 25,380 | LONDON TUESDAY AUGUST 13 1963 | PRICE 3d.

Chief Supt. Ernest Millen

Bandits Got The Breeze-up And Left In A Hurry . . . They Were Ready To Burn Or Bury Their Stuff, Say Yard

YOUR WEATHER

The Meteorological Office states:

6 a.m. TO MIDNIGHT TO-MORROW: Fog patches clearing to give bright intervals, but rather cloudy with scattered showers; wind light, mainly westerly; rather cool, maximum temperature about 19 degrees C., 66 degrees F. OUTLOOK: Continuing rather cool with rain at times but also some bright intervals. CHANNEL: Sea moderate. BAROMETER (2 p.m.): 29.94 in., falling.

Lighting-up time 8.57 p.m. Sun sets 8.27 p.m., rises to-morrow 5.43 a.m. Moon sets 3.35 p.m., rises to-morrow 12.26 a.m. New moon next Monday. High water London Bridge 5.34 a.m., 5.47 p.m. To-morrow 5.43 a.m., 10.10 p.m.

HIDEOUT FOUND

Empty Mailbags And Food In A Lonely Bucks Farmhouse

Yes, The Net Is Closing

"Evening News" Reporter

THE rush by detectives to Leatherslade Farm this afternoon came after a tip from the underworld. The vision of the huge reward was too much for him.

At the same time the police were told the names of six men who were said to have visited the farm recently. All had London addresses.

As soon as the mailbags were discovered the names and addresses were flashed to Scot-

SIX NAMED BY SQUEALER

"EVENING NEWS" REPORTER

THEY'VE FOUND THE HIDEOUT. THAT WAS THE SENSATIONAL MAIL ROBBERY NEWS TO-NIGHT.

Detectives headed by Deputy Commander George Hatherill, of Scotland Yard,

We'll Win Says Mac

STOCKHOLM, Tuesday.

MR. MACMILLAN predicted to-day that the Conservatives will win

CLOSING PRICES

BUS KILLS WOMAN

In Park Royal-road, Acton, Mrs. W Callow (48), of Riverside-gardens, [illegible], fell under a bus and was killed. Motor-cyclist Kenneth Clamp, of East Acton-lane, injured.

THE HIDEOUT

Farm changed hands about a fortnight ago. Mr. B. T. Rixon left to take over a sub post office at Sonning. Keys left with Mrs. Lily Brookes, of Oakley. She said this evening: "A man I had never seen before called on me to collect the keys. He mentioned that he wanted to make a swimming pool in the grounds and told me that he would see me again."

Mr. Rixon said: "I know the name of the man who bought it from me, and his address."

Previous pages: The hideout was Leatherslade Farm. Inset: *Evening News*, 13 August 1963

Opposite: The arrest of Bruce Reynolds

In a recently published book, *No Fixed Address*,[60] ex-Detective Chief Superintendent Frank Williams, who had much to do with the subsequent investigations, claims that at least three men who were directly involved 'are still at liberty and enjoying to the full their share of the money stolen and the profits from the way they invested it'. He says that one of these men was the train driver's assailant, that he traced and identified him and took him to Scotland Yard, but that there was insufficient evidence to charge him.

From this, one may draw two conclusions. First, the judge's statement that 'crime is most certainly not worth the most alluring candle' must have given these 'at least three men' a good laugh. And, secondly, as men known to be guilty of the train robbery but unchargeable with the offence, they must presumably have been under constant police supervision ever since it took place. If none the less they are still at liberty—and one infers that they definitely still were at the time of the publication of Mr Williams's book in 1973—they cannot have put a foot wrong. This must mean that they gave up crime, and could afford to do so on their share of the proceeds from the robbery. But was the judge therefore right in his confident assertion that greed, 'vast greed', was the obvious motive of the crime? One doubts it. Vast greed is, after all, insatiable by its very nature; and if these men have not more recently sought to satisfy it unlawfully, as apparently they have not, they must have done so by legitimate means. But does that seem likely or even possible?

Certainly, Bruce Reynolds, Buster Edwards and James White, who were all three on the run, never, so far as is known, resorted to crime to escape detection, though the two last named badly needed money before the end. White was found living in a caravan in Kent; he said his funds from the robbery were exhausted, and he was thankful the hunt was over. Edwards, who had been to Mexico and Canada among other places, returned to England to surrender. All he had left, according to Mr Williams, who arrested him, was £831, which he handed over to his wife, and a thousand Swiss francs in a Swiss bank.

Reynolds, who had also been in Mexico and Canada, was eventually captured in England on 8 November 1968. Though he was occupying with his wife and young son a fairly luxurious villa overlooking Torquay harbour, Mr Williams says that the money in his case, too, had been 'dwindling'. But Reynolds didn't engage in further

criminal activity to replenish his resources. What appears even more significant is that in August, four months before he was arrested, he took his wife on a sentimental journey to show her the scene of the Great Train Robbery!

Vast greed cannot have been the real motive of these three men. It is conceivable, of course, that they had taken the judge's warning to heart, and refrained from committing another crime out of terror of the additional punishment they'd be certain to receive if they were caught. But it seems far more likely, especially in view of Reynolds's long record set against that extraordinary sentimental journey, that there was a cathartic element in the Great Train Robbery—that those who took part in it, or some of them at least, felt they could never do anything as big or as adventurous again, and for that reason, regardless of whether or not they were able to hang on to the money, would have considered another pettier crime committed in the interest of escaping detection for the 'big job' as something to be scorned.

Ronald Biggs provides, perhaps, the most striking illustration of this theory. Biggs made a dramatic escape over the wall of Wandsworth Prison on 5 January 1965, and after several months in France, where he underwent plastic surgery, he left for Australia. He bought a boarding house in Adelaide, but also had a job as a carpenter, and he continued with this work after he had been joined by his wife and his two sons, though his wife brought him an additional sum of money from his 'capital'. The boarding house was a failure, but Biggs was still working legitimately, though at a higher rate of pay, when he was nearly caught in Melbourne in October 1969 and perforce went on his travels again, leaving his family behind him. Eventually he reached Brazil, where he worked in disguise as a carpenter and interior decorator. He also learned to speak Portuguese, and found a new girlfriend.

After his identity was discovered in 1974, he claimed that he had no money at all left from the robbery. He lived, following his release from custody, in Sepetiba, a small beach town about fifteen miles from Rio de Janeiro, with his girlfriend Raimunda and their baby. It would, of course, have been difficult as well as extremely foolish of him to attempt anything criminal, for he had no legal status in Brazil and had to report twice a week at the local police station. Nevertheless, for years before he had (so far as is known) kept clear of crime, but had earned his living doing carpentry and interior decoration. He was still earning it in the same way, though after his discovery he picked up occasional extras from press, radio and television interviews. In Brazil he became something of a folk hero.

Yet Biggs had a long and formidable criminal record before he took part in the train robbery. Though Peta Fordham in *The Robbers' Tale* says that he was only a labourer, Frank Williams is equally sure that he, along with Reynolds and Goody, was one of the five chieftains who planned the raid, the other two being, presumably, unchargeable. Whichever the case, it would seem that though he had nothing left from the train robbery, it was for him the ultimate crime—the one that, so to speak, forced him to retire, without a penny of savings.

The judge at the original trial may have been right to 'clear out of the way any romantic notions of dare-devilry' and to call the robbery 'nothing less than a sordid crime of violence'.[61] But this is not to say that the robbers themselves (or some of them) did not have a romantic view of what they did or were not proud of having done it. Nor is it at all certain that the acquisition of money—let alone 'vast greed'—was their only or their prime reason for participating in a crime of such immensity.

Mrs Fordham has presented them—and for this much credit is owed to her—not as a bunch of criminals, but as individual human beings; she has tried to explain rather than excuse their behaviour. They were some of them, in her view, extremely intelligent, and were quite obviously none of them out of their minds in a legal or medical sense. I find it surprising, though, that she should describe James Hussey as belonging to a 'pretty dumb' group, for though I have never met him, I had a letter from him after he had been made editor of the Hull prison periodical—a post which he held only briefly. His letter was admirably phrased and written in a remarkably beautiful hand. Mrs Fordham describes Biggs as being 'not very bright', but, again, I got rather the opposite impression from his performance during a television interview.

Charles Wilson, for whose brain Mrs Fordham has considerable respect, had escaped from prison before she published her book, and was not recaptured until three years afterwards, in January 1968. Interestingly enough, she had predicted that he would 'either reform or run to permanent ruin', and in fact he did appear to have reformed during his absence without leave. He settled with his wife and three children (to whom he was devoted) in a four-bedroom house he had built on a half-acre site at Mountain View, Rigaud, Quebec Province, Canada. He joined the local golf club, and was about to join a

Opposite: *Evening Standard*, 16 April 1964

local charity that helped handicapped children, for one of his own children had a hole in the heart. He owned a car, two dogs and a cat, and his two elder children attended the local high school. In short, he was leading a perfectly normal life under the name of Alloway at the time he was caught and brought back to England.

He was not especially extravagant. His house had cost him £11,000 in cash together with a £7,000 mortgage. Thirty-four thousand dollars were found in his home after his arrest as well as jewels and other valuables worth about £14,000. It would be purely conjectural to say whether he will still be 'reformed' when he is finally released. He will be 51 unless he is granted parole meanwhile, and his children will be children no longer.

Mrs Fordham believes that Goody, like the compulsive gambler whose unconscious desire is not to win money but to lose it, was in crime because he wanted, without knowing it, to be caught. And she says that he would have done any job, however great or small the potential reward, simply for the excitement of doing it. This is reminiscent, it will be remembered, of what Joe Redenbaugh thought of himself twenty years after he had been sent to Stillwater, and why he still believed he might have reverted to stealing if he'd been released. 'Just the excitement probably. More the excitement and one thing and another like that than the actual money. Going out and doin' somethin' that was over and above what the ordinary guy could do.'

To say what will happen to Goody now is a matter of prediction which may be proved false by the time this book appears. He may have reformed himself, if he is made of the same tough fibre as Joseph Redenbaugh. I think it very unlikely that prison will have reformed him. Nor can I begin to guess how much he, or any of the others, will have left of the money they stole. Other considerations apart, when one remembers inflation, it seems unlikely to be a fortune.

The saddest among the train robbers was William Boal. He had, according to Mrs Fordham, no motive at all for the crime, because he was wrongly convicted. (I had similar information from an inside prison source.) He had a criminal record, was closely associated, even in the spending spree, with Cordrey, but had been going straight since 1949 and had built up a tiny business in precision engineering. All he could have looked forward to during his twenty-four-year sentence was one day to get back to his workshop. But this was denied him. He died in prison.

WEST END FINAL

Evening Standard

43,490 THURSDAY, APRIL 16, 1964 ● ● 3d. 5

'The game is not worth even the most alluring candle'

ROY JAMES—30 years

DOUGLAS GOODY—30 years

CHARLES WILSON—30 years

THOMAS WISBEY—30 years

RONALD BIGGS—30 years

ROBERT WELCH—30 years

SEVEN GET 30 YEARS EACH

the GREAT TRAIN ROBBERY

AMES HUSSEY—30 years

BRIAN FIELD—25 years

EONARD FIELD—25 years

ILLIAM BOAL—24 years

GER CORDREY—20 years

N WHEATER—Three years

Sentences total 307 years

Evening Standard Reporter: Aylesbury, Thursday

It was the crime of the century . . . the £2,517,975 raid on a mail train in the 3 a.m. darkness of Buckinghamshire. And today came the reckoning: 307 years in jail for 12 of the men involved.

Sentences on all counts totalled 573 years but because they were concurrent the period of imprisonment was cut by 266 years.

It took Mr. Justice Edmund Davies 32 minutes to pass the sentences at Aylesbury.

A WINK . . . A 'THANK YOU'

Seven of the men found guilty of taking part in the raid and conspiracy were each jailed for 30 years.

They were Ronald Arthur Biggs, Douglas Gordon Goody, Charles Frederick Wilson, Thomas William Wisbey, Robert Welch, James Hussey and Roy John James.

The other sentences ranged from 25 to three years.

The 12 men heard their sentences calmly.

Biggs, a slight smile on his face, winked at his wife as he left the dock. Wisbey drummed his fingers on the dock rail but gave no sign of emotion. Wilson paled . . . and said nothing.

Welch worked his mouth as if he was chewing gum. Then he bowed low.

From Hussey came an almost inaudible "Thank you, your Honour." James held his hands clasped behind his back.

Goody, grim-faced, gave a toss of his head and clenched his fists as he was led away.

'OH, MY POOR BOY'

The only outburst came when Leonard Field, 31, was sentenced to 25 years for conspiracy.

His 73-year-old mother, a grey-haired tiny figure in a black velvet coat with fur collar screamed: "Oh, my poor boy . . ."

As she was led out Field called out: "Never mind, mother. I am still young."

Mr. Justice Edmund Davies told the court that to deal with the charges leniently would be an evil thing.

Saying that the crime was the first of its kind in the

● Back Page, Col. Three

WEATHER—Warm.—See Page 17.

❝ This conduct constitutes a menace to society . . . It is nothing less than a sordid crime of violence inspired by vast greed . . .

The consequence of this outrageous crime is that the vast booty of £2,500,000 remains almost entirely unrecovered.

It would be an affront if you were to be at liberty in the near future to enjoy these ill-gotten gains. I propose to secure that such an opportunity will be denied to you for an extremely long time. ❞

MR. JUSTICE EDMUND DAVIES, THE JUDGE AT THE MAIL ROBBERY TRIAL TODAY.

Royal wedding in September

COPENHAGEN, Thursday. — King Constantine of Greece and Princess Anne-Marie of Denmark will marry in Athens on September 18, the Danish court announced today.

'Ferranti company beat Whitehall'

The MPs' "watchdog" committee on public accounts reported today on the Ferranti contract.

The committee find that:

THE COMPANY was able to beat Whitehall's technical costs estimate by "an enormous margin"; and

THE MINISTRY—"one of the most disturbing facts"—had not been able to establish how it happened.

The MPs consider that the firm made an "excessive profit." This was contested by Mr. Sebastian de Ferranti, the chairman and managing director.

Fuller report—Page FIVE.

New plans to beat the dopers

PAGE TWENTY

PART 5
FRAUD
1/Victor Lustig

The fraud in our society ranges all the way from the out-and-out 'con man' to the big business tycoon who gambles against the law and loses. The former is usually, perhaps, the more 'honest' of the two—at least with himself.

Opposite: 'Count' Victor Lustig, professional con man, whose greatest con, probably was to have persuaded the police that he had sold the Eiffel Tower

'Count' Victor Lustig, who probably had a greater number of aliases than he himself could remember, was finally convicted on a counterfeiting charge and sent to Alcatraz for twenty years: a sentence which his death interrupted. Before that, however, as Governor Lehmann of New York pointed out in an address on 30 September 1935, Lustig, though he had been arrested at least twenty-three times in eleven different states, had never been sent to prison in the U.S.A. Yet, as the Governor also remarked, in central Europe, where his criminal career began in 1908, he had been arrested eight times for such offences as theft, embezzlement and swindling, and on each occasion had suffered a more or less short term of imprisonment. This, in Governor Lehmann's opinion, was proof of the deterrent effectiveness of prison, and explained why Lustig had in 1917 transferred his activities to the United States.

Since his last trial there was also his first, it is impossible to know for certain much else about the crimes he committed or was accused of committing. But he evidently proved such a remarkably forthcoming source of information about his own misdoings that James F. Johnson, a former agent of America's Secret Service (which deals with counterfeiting, among other things), was able to write a book, in collaboration with Floyd Miller of the *Reader's Digest,* called *The Man Who Sold the Eiffel Tower.*[62]

The decorative dialogue in this book, of which there is a prodigious amount, is presumably largely, if not exclusively, owed to the imagination of Mr Miller. But Lustig must clearly be the source of most of the facts. One would like to believe them true, in particular the story that gives the book its title.

This tells of Lustig's arrival in Paris in May 1925, when he put up at the Crillon Hotel and was greeted by the room clerk with deference as Count Lustig. (That is important to note.) He was accompanied by 'Dapper' Dan Collins whom he introduced as Monsieur Dante. Dapper Dan Collins was a fellow rogue: reputedly handsome, well dressed and a French linguist.

Lustig read in the paper that the Eiffel Tower was in need of very costly repairs, and this gave him his idea of the 'mark'. Five men were invited by the Deputy Director of the Ministry of Posts and Telegraphs, on forged writing paper, of course, to attend a meeting in a suite at the Crillon Hotel (though how the reception desk was squared is not explained). Among them was the 'mark', André Poisson. Lustig, posing as the Deputy Director, thanked them all for coming, and then told them the reason why they had been invited. It was, he said, a state secret known only to his Director, the Premier of France and President Doumergue, but the government had decided to scrap the Eiffel Tower. It was for sale.

Lustig took them in limousines on a tour of inspection, and contrived to get them into the tower itself for nothing by flashing phoney credentials at the guard. Then he asked the five men to send their bids in sealed envelopes to the Crillon Hotel by the following week.

The bids arrived, and Dapper Dan, still in the person of Monsieur Dante, went to call on the 'mark'—a man of peasant origin who had had great success in the scrap iron business through his energy and drive—to tell him his bid was successful. Poisson requested a weekend to raise the money, and on the following Tuesday he was once more ushered into Lustig's suite. (Again, it is not explained how the reception desk, which knew Lustig as Count Lustig, was squared.) Poisson seemed suspicious until Lustig, after instructing Dapper Dan to return to the 'Bureau', told him the reason why this business was being conducted unofficially at the Crillon instead of officially at the Bureau. It was that the Deputy Director, times being so hard and his expenses so heavy, expected a 'commission'. Poisson roared with happy laughter. This was talk he understood, and he was more than satisfied. He handed over a substantial bribe in notes and also produced his cheque for the Eiffel Tower. Later, of course, he realized he had been conned, but he never said a word about it for fear of being made the laughing-stock of Paris.

This story is retold in a chapter from a book called *Great Swindlers* by A. F. L. Deeson (M.A., Ph.D., D.Sc.) published in London in 1971. There are some variations—for example, Dan Collins disappears and Lustig himself becomes Monsieur Dante—but the decorative dialogue is in places word for word the same as Miller's; and it seems most unlikely that Deeson can have been in touch with the original source in order to make his alterations and adjustments to the story, for Lustig died in 1947. It is indeed a good story, and, as has been said, one would like to believe it. But there are several gaping holes in it, apart from the one already mentioned and which Deeson avoids. For instance, what of Poisson's four competitors? Weren't any of them suspicious? And what of the cheque which was allegedly cashed at the Bank of France? Johnson and Miller say it was 'certified', without realizing, perhaps, that a certified cheque is known only in America. Deeson, on the other hand, says that it was made out on Lustig's insistence to 'Monsieur Banchard'. And one could go on.

It seems equally unlikely that Lustig ever met Al Capone, as Johnson and Miller claim. A story in the *New York Times* of 6 July 1929 reveals that Lustig (alias Robert V. Miller) and a man called William McSherry of Philadelphia had been arrested and held by the Paris police, after being found with a dozen or more false passports in their luggage. They claimed to be agents of Al Capone. They had, they said, been having difficulty in disposing of Capone's stocks in Paris, and were therefore going on to Prague. But the police in Chicago, when interviewed by a reporter, were unable to trace any connection between either of them and Capone's gang.

In any case, Lustig's own story of his association with Al Capone, or the one relayed by Johnson and Miller, was different and far more romantic. It was that he had called on the gang leader at his headquarters in Chicago, taken $50,000 from him on the understanding that he would double it, then after a lapse of sixty days had returned the money intact, and had been rewarded by Al Capone with $5,000 for his nerve in trying to make a 'mark' out of him (and, of course, succeeding!).

Lustig may have found his inspiration for this story in the rumour (it was certainly no more than a rumour) that Capone was an enemy of the New York gangster Jack 'Legs' Diamond, because he had handed him $75,000 to gamble in the casino at Monte Carlo and had received only $20,000 in return. For undoubtedly Lustig was, during a short period at least, associated with Diamond, though in what way precisely it is impossible to be sure. On 20 October 1930 the *New York Times* and the *Herald Tribune* both reported that a 'Count' Duval, alias Robert V. Miller, had been questioned by the police about the shooting of Diamond at the Hotel Monticello in New York. The *Herald Tribune* got the impression that he was 'something of a private secretary' to Diamond, and it reported that he had been planning to go to Germany in Diamond's place, or as his representative, to arrange for a shipment of rye whisky. It said, furthermore, that last year (1929) Diamond and 'Count' Duval had been arrested on a hold-up charge in Newark, that this year

Duval had been arrested on a grand larceny charge in Atlantic City and released on $5,000 bail, and finally that Duval was at present conferring in New Bedford, Massachusetts, on an unspecified charge that was pending in Boston.

The *New York Times* report varied in parts, and added some details. It said that 'Count' Duval, alias Robert V. Miller, had first met Diamond some three years ago at a cabaret in Paris. He agreed to go to Germany to arrange the rye whisky shipment, but Diamond had travelled there ahead of him, and as he was about to debark he learned that Diamond had been arrested and was being held on suspicion. So this changed his plans, and he hurried on to Paris, where he borrowed $200 from a lawyer friend. A few days later he received a telegram from Diamond, telling him to get in touch with a man called Burkhardt in London, who owed him (Diamond) money. After searching London in vain for Burkhardt, he returned to New York, and saw Diamond again on 7 October (1930) at the Monticello Hotel.

How much can be believed of either of these reports one does not know, but it is at least true presumably that a 'Count' Duval (alias Miller) was questioned about the Diamond shooting in October 1930, and there is no doubt that 'Count' Lustig, 'Count' Duval and Robert V. Miller were one and the same person.

Johnson and Miller tell a far more colourful story about Lustig's association with Diamond: according to their version, both men were working for the gambler Arnold Rothstein. He sent them to Paris on a narcotics mission, but this failed because Diamond was stopped from entering France by the French police. Diamond returned, fuming with rage, to New York's Monticello Hotel, where he was later joined by Lustig. Lustig treated him with aristocratic disdain, until Diamond said, 'What are we gonna tell Arnold?' That got Lustig really scared—the thought of the vengeance the powerful Arnold Rothstein could take on them.

Johnson and Miller go on to relate how Diamond was shot the very same night, and how Lustig 'bolted', catching 'the first train out of town'. But here, apart from the fact that Lustig must still have been in town when he was questioned by the police, they are a little confused (as, indeed, they are elsewhere) about dates. For the Diamond shooting at the Monticello Hotel happened in 1930; that is to say, two years after 'Arnold' had been murdered.

The truth is that Lustig didn't make any headlines in

New York, or attract more than an occasional paragraph on an inside page, until the counterfeiting case in 1935. Then the newspapers described him as an 'internationally known swindler', but they had said little to justify this reputation beforehand. In 1921 the *New York Times* carried a report (which, unfortunately, it failed to follow up) that Missouri was trying to get Lustig extradited from Kansas. Lustig had been to the American Savings Bank in Springfield and informed the cashier, Bert Ellis, of his wish to buy some land. He was told that the bank itself owned a ranch, and he accordingly negotiated to buy the ranch with liberty bonds on the understanding that the bank would pay him the difference in cash—it amounted to $16,000—between the purchase price and the total value of his bonds. Eventually he got away with both bonds and cash, though how was not adequately explained. Strangely enough, the informant of his whereabouts in Kansas was said to be his 'wife', for there is no reference anywhere else to his ever having been married (at least as far as I have been able to discover), though there is much that Johnson and Miller have to say about his success with, and exploitation of, women.

They give a considerably more elaborate version of the Missouri Savings Bank story: in fact, they change 'all the names and places', because when they went to question the sons of the bank officials concerned (the officials themselves being long since dead), the sons denied all knowledge of Lustig but their eyes revealed 'pain and fear'. Briefly, Johnson and Miller say that Lustig was able to convince the bank's lawyer, who in turn convinced the bank, that its depositors would withdraw their money if they ever knew how easily its officers had been conned. But in fact, of course, considering the public demand for Lustig's extradition, it is clear that the depositors must already have been exactly aware of what had happened and that no effort was ever made to keep it secret from them.

The first time that Johnson met Lustig was in 1935 after Lustig's arrest in New York as the prime mover in the distribution of counterfeit money; and it was then that Lustig told him (and the other arresting officers) so candidly and apparently so imaginatively about so many of his exploits. He even asked permission to go to a hotel where a 'mark' was waiting to give him $10,000. This request was understandably refused, and instead one of the officers was sent along to inform the 'mark' that he had just avoided being swindled. The 'mark' was furious, not with Lustig, in whom he still had complete faith, but with the men who he was convinced had spoiled his chance of making some easy money.

Here Johnson is speaking from his own knowledge, and one believes him. Nor does one doubt that Lustig must have been a remarkably capable and resourceful cheat. Not long after his arrest he escaped from the federal House of Detention wearing prison clothes and in full view of the lunchtime passers-by He cut his way through the screen of the upper dormitory window—how he managed to do this was never discovered—and could be plainly observed for a few minutes standing on the ledge, engaged in vigorous cleaning operations. Then the cloth he was using snaked down to earth—it was in reality a rope made from sheets tied together—and he descended, landing on his hands and knees, though without apparently hurting himself, for he was quickly on his feet again. The audience that had gathered to watch this extraordinary spectacle was flabbergasted, and not one of them thought to inform the police or alert the prison guards until it was too late. Lustig gave a little bow, and was off. Twenty-eight days passed before he was re-arrested in Pittsburgh. He was brought back to New York, and this time placed in the Tombs for safekeeping.

According to the New York press, he was known as the 'Count' in, and apparently only in, the underworld. He was described as an ashen-faced man of 45, with a scar running from his left eyebrow to his left ear, who spoke with a 'continental accent'. Among his favourite methods of swindling was said to be the use of something he called his money box. He claimed (so the press reports went on) that the money box did not counterfeit, but actually reproduced dollar bills by some secret chemical process, and since he had invariably fixed things in advance he could call on a bank after a demonstration to

'Count' Lustig Is Seized in Pittsburgh; Federal Agents Block Flight to Chicago

Special to THE NEW YORK TIMES.

PITTSBURGH, Pa., Sept. 28.—"Count" Victor Lustig was arrested here today by Department of Justice and Secret Service agents who have been on his trail since Sept. 1, when he escaped from the Federal House of Detention in New York, where he had been held since May as the leader of a gang of counterfeiters.

C. K. Fierstone, head of the De-

Last May, however, they nabbed him as he opened a Times Square subway locker. In the locker were $150,000 in cleverly manufactured counterfeit bills and the dies from which they had been made.

Lustig is also known as Robert V. Miller.

By The Associated Press.

PITTSBURGH, Sept. 28.—Federal records made public here today de-

New York Times, 29 September 1935

prove his claim. His 'marks' included a sheriff who had arrested him on a charge of fraud. He gave the sheriff a demonstration and sold him the box in return for his freedom and a tidy sum of money.

Once again, Johnson and Miller relate this story with a wealth of additional detail. They say that the sheriff caught up with Lustig in a Chicago hotel six months after he'd been conned, and threatened him with a gun. Lustig remained quite unmoved. 'Did you', so the decorative dialogue runs, 'turn the sequential knob twice to the right and then back to point ten at the left? Then move the additive switch ten seconds later? Exactly ten seconds, not nine or eleven? Then the three-stage inductive knob *before* you turned the compressor?'

'For Christ's sake, I don't know. All I know is it won't work.'

Thereupon, say Johnson and Miller, Lustig graciously handed the sheriff ten thousand dollars in notes, saying he would reclaim the amount when he could afford the time to make the journey to Oklahoma and teach him how to use the box. Four days later, while still in Chicago, he was relieved to read in a New Orleans newspaper which he had been careful to buy (but why this Oklahoma official should have gone to New Orleans is left unexplained) that the sheriff had been arrested and charged with passing counterfeit notes. Johnson and Miller add that he was subsequently convicted and sent to the federal penitentiary in Lewisburg, Pennsylvania. If that is true rather than another invention of Lustig's, one may wonder why such a fiery fellow as the sheriff is alleged to have been should not have denounced the real counterfeiter rather than meekly allowing himself to be railroaded into prison.

There was speculation in the New York press as to whether Lustig might be identical with the mysterious 'Count' Corrigan, who had figured briefly, and then completely vanished, in the Jules 'Nicky' Arnstein case of 1920. According to the evidence, the 'Count' (posing as a U.S. marshall) visited the store owned by Joseph Gluck's father—Joseph Gluck was head of the messenger boys who stole securities for Arnstein—and extorted from him a car, a diamond ring, $2,000 in cash and $85,000 worth of securities. While Johnson and Miller do not mention this particular incident, they go much further in connecting Lustig with Arnstein. For Lustig, they say, learned the subtleties of 'marksmanship' from Arnstein on a pre-World War I transatlantic cruise. Whether or not this is true—and it would seem to conflict with

Governor Lehmann's information that Lustig only arrived in America in 1917—Lustig himself or Arnstein were the only possible sources of the story, and in view of the fact that as far as is known Johnson never met Arnstein, it must have been Lustig.

At his trial in New York in December 1935, the assistant U.S. attorney told the court that from July 1930 to 1935 he and the engraver had created and distributed $2,340,000 in counterfeit notes. The engraver, a man named Watts, started to give evidence for the prosecution, but Lustig intervened before he had got very far with a plea of guilty. 'All I wanted to see', the *New York Times* reported him as saying, 'was whether the rat would squeal on the stand.'

Lustig got twenty years, and there his story ends, except for his death certificate in 1947, which simply records that he was born in Hostinne, Czechoslovakia, that he had no social security number, and that his usual occupation was 'apprentice salesman'.

But conceivably the reason why he put up such a shabbily feeble fight for freedom at the last was that he felt himself fulfilled. It seems virtually certain that he told Johnson and his co-agents a succession of fantasticated or romanticized accounts of his career in crime. One can hardly believe that the newspapers would have missed telling the Eiffel Tower story, when he was big news, if they'd ever heard of it. What is more, he was a Czech, and, if the press spoke the truth, he still spoke English after years in America with a 'continental accent'. But he must have had perfect French to sell the Eiffel Tower to Monsieur Poisson, and, incidentally, entertain four others to champagne and truffles without arousing their deepest suspicions.

Maybe he wanted to be remembered as the supreme gentleman crook of all time; and that, though they call him pitiless, is pretty well what Johnson and Miller represent him to have been: a man possessed of dazzling charm and immense erudition, who spent money like water, was impeccably dressed, employed a liveried chauffeur, and, in the popular imagination, was every inch the count that he now and then pretended to be.

From a report in the *New York Herald Tribune,* 1 May 1935: '"Count", said one of the agents, "you're the smoothest man that ever lived."

'"I wouldn't say that", said the prisoner smiling, "after all, you have conned me."'

Had he been conned? Or was it his final and best con to assure himself of a memorial larger than life?

FRAUD

2/Horatio Bottomley, Clarence Hatry, Leopold Harris

Horatio Bottomley was possibly the greatest and certainly the most distinguished swindler of the century. He was not only a dishonest company tycoon, but was also what amounted to a con man, with a superabundance of the con man's charm and persuasiveness. For example, in partnership with Ernest Hooley, another rogue who was also one of his passionate admirers, he robbed an old man named George Masters of his entire fortune, something over £130,000, by selling him totally worthless shares.

Bottomley's motive was, as the train robbers' pretty certainly was not, vast greed—at least on the conscious level. However much money he had at any one time—and he earned enormous sums—it was never enough; he was forever in debt, and on four occasions was made bankrupt. His tastes, too, were reflective of his greed. He came from a poor and humble background; and he enjoyed all the things he thought money should buy, such as racehorses, women and quantities of champagne.

But Bottomley was a great deal else besides being a fraud. He had a dazzling array of talents. He was a spellbinding public speaker, a brilliantly successful editor of the periodical *John Bull* and the highest-paid journalist in Britain, a backer of plays, including Forbes Robertson's immortal *Hamlet,* an outstandingly successful amateur lawyer, who could enlist the sympathy of judges as well as mesmerize juries, and, during the First World War, a sort of professional but immensely effective patriot. He was also twice elected Member of Parliament for South Hackney; and on the second occasion, after the surrender of Germany, there was a rumour (to which he himself gave full credit) that he would be invited to join Lloyd George's cabinet. It is not altogether surprising that his fall was front-page news in the *New York Times,* though he hardly knew America.

Bottomley was first tried for fraud in 1893. He defended himself, and was acquitted with the wholehearted approval of Mr Justice Hawkins, despite the latter's deserved reputation as a 'hanging judge'. A succession of court appearances followed, but it was not until June 1922, nearly forty years later, that he was finally unmasked. Bottomley was then 62, and again he defended

The Star, 22 February 1922

Below: Horatio Bottomley, 'I Have Paid BUT . . .'

BOTTOMLEY ACCUSED OF CONVERTING FUNDS.

SUMMONS SERVED TO-DAY: TRIP TO PARIS CANCELLED.

BOW-STREET HEARING ON MARCH 8.

SIR ARCHIBALD BODKIN, Director of Public Prosecutions, applied in person to Mr. Chester Jones, the Bow-street magistrate, yesterday, and was granted a summons against Mr. Horatio Bottomley, M.P.

The application was made privately. Mr. Bottomley read the news to-day, and rang up Scotland Yard to inform the authorities that—

He had intended to go to Paris this week on business, but in view of the statement in the press that the Public Prosecutor was issuing a summons against him, he had cancelled the journey.

CHARGE OF CONVERSION.

The summons was served on him at 12.50 this afternoon.

He is charged with converting to his own use £5,000, part of the property of the Victory Bond Club, on September 16, 1919.

himself—this time on charges of fraudulently converting to his own use money that had been entrusted to him by members of the public as a result of a scheme announced in *John Bull* for investment in the Victory Bond Club, among other enterprises of a similar kind. According to Travers Humphreys, who prosecuted him, Bottomley was a mere drink-sodden relic of what he once had been, but he still made a characteristically powerful and emotional closing speech, and it was doubtless a misfortune for him that this came on Friday afternoon so that the jury was allowed a whole weekend to recover from its effects. Furthermore, the judge's summing-up (charge) this time proved to be extremely adverse, and the jury took less than half an hour to find the defendant guilty.

Although Bottomley had, in fact, under mounting pressure, returned much of the money entrusted to him, it is virtually certain that the judge's sentencing speech was fully justified. 'Horatio Bottomley', he said, 'you have been rightly convicted by the jury of this long series of heartless frauds. These poor people trusted you, and you robbed them of £150,000 in ten months.'[63]

Equally, it is true that he had escaped imprisonment before only through his remarkable powers of advocacy, combined with a certain amount of luck, and understandably none of his biographers has attempted to deny this or to whitewash him. But one wonders, just the same, whether it was the 'truth' for Bottomley himself—whether he was honest in his flagrant dishonesty or whether his vanity, which was colossal, convinced him, even in his innermost private thoughts, that he could not conceivably be a common fraud?

There is evidence on both sides. On the one hand, the first Lord Birkenhead, who had much admiration for Bottomley as a Member of Parliament, was none the less aware of his reputation, and on one occasion, when a new Archbishop of Canterbury was about to be enthroned, didn't hesitate to tell him so. 'You ought to go along there, Horatio', he said, 'he needs a crook.' And Bottomley appeared to relish this *bon mot* at his expense.[64]

On the other hand, after his sentence to seven years' penal servitude, he wrote a letter from the hospital at Wormwood Scrubs prison to the Speaker of the House of Commons, which read as follows: 'I desire, first of all, Sir, to express my sorrow at having brought this slur upon the House of Commons, which I can honestly say I have loved, as I have loved my country and my King.'[65]

Presumably he intended this reference to his love for

King and Country to remind members of his wartime speeches which had won him the reputation, at least among those poor people whom he subsequently robbed, of being second to none in patriotic fervour and devotion. He certainly could not have meant to imply any admission of guilt, for he went on to deny it specifically: 'I am the victim of an appalling error of justice.'

Did he really mean this? Was he, in his own peculiar way, being sincere? When I was about 16, I remember hearing Arthur Comyns Carr, who subjected Bottomley to a devastating cross-examination in the case that led to his prosecution, tell how his patriotism was a mere cover for coining money—how at a meeting he'd exchange a knowing wink with his manager. Alan Hyman, whose *The Rise and Fall of Horatio Bottomley* was published in 1972, says that from the winter of 1915 for the following three years, though he refused to take any money for his recruiting speeches, because he hated the thought of sending young men to their deaths, these numbered only 20; whereas during the same period he delivered 340 'patriotic lectures' up and down the country, and drew £25 for each of them from *John Bull* as well as discreetly demanding between 75 and 85 per cent of the gate. So there is no doubt that he grew richer and fatter on his 'patriotism'; and one would be justified in concluding that if this was phoney, so, too, was his protestation of innocence.

Yet one may also believe that neither was. For it is surely a mistaken idea to assume that everyone who swears he did something that he obviously didn't, or didn't do something that he obviously did, is automatically a liar, except objectively. He may be, as for example Crippen probably was, a huge fantasist. And in Bottomley's case certainly it is difficult to explain his behaviour after he had been released from prison at the end of July 1927, except on the grounds of gross self-delusion.

I can still recall the huge posters announcing the publication of a series of articles in the *Weekly Dispatch*, 'I Have Paid BUT . . .' by Horatio Bottomley. Readers of the *Weekly Dispatch*—I was not one of them, for at 16 I was too young to know much if anything about Bottomley in the days before his imprisonment—learned that the 'BUT' was followed by 'I Did Not Owe The Debt'.

The series began immediately after Bottomley's release as a ticket of leave man in July 1927, and continued, dwindlingly, until the end of the year. Read today, it has next to nothing to recommend it. There is too much second-rate doggerel quoted from what Bottomley called his *Songs of the Cell,* and very little serious attempt to outline a programme of penal reform. But Bottomley was paid an enormous sum for it: £12,000, the equivalent of at least £144,000 at the time of writing, and subject to far less tax.

Why did he throw away this last opportunity to live a secure, comfortable, if relatively modest life at The Dicker, the country estate which he owned? The point is not that he should once again have denied his guilt so vigorously. That is something he might well have felt obliged to do, even though he was fully aware of it, in the interests of telling a good story. Nor by the same token is it a wonder that he should have told the editor of the *Weekly Dispatch* that all he could think about during his five years in prison was his innocence!

But even if he was secretly capable of facing the truth about himself, he must surely have realized that he could never hope for another chance to earn money on a similar scale, or hope for a resurgence of his former fame. He had shot his bolt. Cheque book journalism—and that was all it was—had rewarded him more handsomely than it had rewarded anyone before, or would do again, but still left him as nothing more than a blown crook. He should have settled for obscurity.

There is no evidence that he spent a penny on making good the losses (suffered, he of course said, through no fault of his) of Victory Bond holders, though he had promised loudly that he would repay every one of them in full. (It had been a favourite trick of his to offer to recompense a sucker who had lost money in one of his companies and then fleece him of some more.) But he made costly efforts at a comeback, which eventually resulted in his fourth bankruptcy and lost him The Dicker. Notably, there was the publication of *John Blunt* in 1928, which, with its declared devotion to the interests of the common man, was supposed to bring back memories of his editorship of *John Bull.* It collapsed after a few weeks. Nobody could take Bottomley seriously any longer, because nobody trusted him. And it was this fact that foredoomed all his attempts at a comeback to failure.

In 1932 he was advertised as one of the items in a non-stop revue at London's Windmill Theatre, telling anecdotes of his past, and out of curiosity I went to see him. He had always been a little man, but at the time of his imprisonment he was hugely fat—blown out by his quantities of champagne. Now, as he shuffled on to the stage, he was shrunk almost to nothing, and his whole appearance totally lacked strength or buoyancy; it was

MILLIONAIRE AT 30 —CONVICT TO-DAY.

THE AMAZING CAREER OF CLARENCE HATRY.

HIS GERMAN PARENTS.

WIFE COLLAPSES ON HEARING THE SENTENCE.

PRISONERS.	SENTENCES.
Clarence Hatry, aged forty-two, financier and ex-millionaire, of Stanhope-street and Pinners Hall.	Fourteen years penal servitude, two periods of five years, and two years hard labour, to run concurrently.
Edmund Daniels, aged thirty-two, a company director.	Seven years' penal servitude, two periods of five years and two years' hard labour, to run concurrently.
Albert Edward Tabor, thirty-six, a director.	Three years' penal servitude and two years' hard labour, to run concurrently.
John Graham Goodfellow Dixon, thirty-seven, company secretary.	Two periods of five years' penal servitude and two years hard labour, to run concurrently.

Those sentences, passed by Mr. Justice Avory at the Old Bailey yesterday, wrote "finis" to the sensational frauds and forgeries involving £2,000,000 of money which have been committed by Clarence Hatry and his three fellow-directors of the Austin Friars Trust, of Pinners Hall, in the City of London.

The sentences also smashed the career of one of the most spectacular figures in the City—Clarence Hatry, born of German parents, his father a merchant of Hampstead, the man who rose from obscurity to wealth and power and who handled millions of money before he was thirty years of age.

"ARABIAN NIGHTS" MANSION.

He owned racehorses, splendid yachts, and a mansion in Mayfair described as "something out of the 'Arabian Nights.'"

He rolled on his heels like a drunken man yesterday when he heard the words "*fourteen years*," turned to go, and was stopped to hear an additional sentence. He left the dock, to be called back for a second time by the judge, who said: "Bring him back, I had forgotten the third indictment."

Mrs. Hatry completely collapsed when she was told of the sentences imposed on her husband.

"THE MAN WHO ALWAYS PAID."

merely old and pathetic. Yet, although I can remember nothing of what he said, he was able to hold my attention; and I could easily imagine what magnetism he must once have possessed.

Actually, though I don't recall hearing anything about this at the time, his engagement at the Windmill Theatre was cut short when he collapsed midway through a performance. He was nearing the end of his life, and was forced to live the short rest of it on the charity of a devoted woman friend, a former chorus girl named Peggy Primrose. His wife Eliza, who was anyway useless to him, had died at The Dicker in 1930, and his daughter Florence, of whom he was very fond, had gone to live in South Africa with her second husband. Peggy Primrose was the only one, among his dozens of mistresses, whom he loved and who loved him, though conscious of all his faults, in return.

One suspects that other financiers who gambled too often against the law may have been, like Bottomley, fantasists. But if so, Clarence Hatry was an exception. In 1930 he received twice as long a sentence as had been imposed on Bottomley for a morally less reprehensible offence. The fraud that he committed was admittedly gigantic, but it involved banks and financial houses rather than poor people.

Hatry could have stayed within the law by allowing his companies to crash and forgoing the opportunity to create a giant steel corporation out of which he stood to make millions. He preferred (or, as it was said by his counsel at the trial, he yielded to the insistence of an Italian fellow director who had since found refuge in his homeland) the terrible risk of raising some £822,000 from various banks, including the Equitable Trust Company of New York, by means of forged scrip. The gamble failed, and Hatry went immediately to the police along with his English fellow directors They provided the evidence upon which the extremely complicated case against them was prepared, although they were all refused bail.

It was a misfortune for Hatry that he came before Mr Justice Avory, who had the reputation of being incomparably severe. It was also a misfortune that his fraud had been committed at a time when the world was engulfed in a crisis, and nothing seemed more likely, as the prosecutor said, to hinder the restoration of Britain's prosperity than this robbery of financial institutions. 'You stand convicted on your own confession of the most appalling frauds that have ever disfigured the commercial

Opposite above left: Clarence Hatry in Paris after his release from prison in 1939

Right: Hatry's house in Great Stanhope Street, London, where he lived before his conviction

Left: *Daily Express,* 25 January 1930

reputation of the country', the judge said in passing sentence, 'frauds far more serious than any of the great frauds upon the public which have been committed within the last fifty years according to my personal experience. Stripped of its rhetoric, the excuse put forward on your behalf is nothing more than the threadbare belief of every clerk and servant who robs his master when he says he hoped to repay the money by backing a winner.'[66]

Those last words did not represent an original thought on the part of Mr Justice Avory. More or less the same thing had been said to Bottomley when he was sentenced. And though it was obviously true as far as it went, Mr Justice Avory might have considered what the position would have been if Hatry's gamble had come off. As a matter of fact, it very nearly did; and other big business tycoons had undoubtedly (in the fashion of servant robbing master) resorted to some kind of extra-legal action without anyone being any the wiser.

The *Daily Express* of London said that Hatry 'reeled' in the dock when he was sentenced to fourteen years. The *New York Times,* on the other hand, remarked on the extraordinary stolidity and calm of both Hatry and his fellow directors, who received lesser punishments. 'It was as if these stoic men had, as one observer remarked, sworn a compact that the world outside should never know their thoughts and should never see their hearts.'[67] One does not know which of these two accounts to believe. Hatry must obviously have been prepared for a fairly stiff prison sentence, but not for one as long as fourteen years, since he appealed against it. His appeal was dismissed, the Lord Chief Justice remarking that the sentence wasn't 'a day too long'.

Hatry had owned yachts, racehorses, and a fabulous mansion in Mayfair. But, unlike Bottomley, and for that matter most big-time financiers who have come to grief, he was abstemious and a devoted family man. Greed was not his motive; he pursued money for the sake of pursuing it; and he worked some fourteen hours a day at this task. Luxuries, home and extravagance, he simply regarded as the proof of his success. He gained nothing personally from his frauds; on the contrary, he invested his entire fortune in the effort to stave off disaster, and was made a bankrupt after the crash. But it was his singlemindedness, his devotion to the art of making money, that no doubt enabled him to stage a minor comeback in the bookselling business after he was released from prison in 1939. He wasn't, despite the harsh words the judges had used about him, a man who could never be trusted again.

One would have supposed that if there was anyone of whom this could *not* be said it was Leopold Harris, who in 1933 suffered the same fate as Clarence Hatry—fourteen years' penal servitude. Harris was not a financier. He had inherited a fire assessor's firm from his father, and to an extent he practised this business quite legitimately, with skill and perseverance. But he was also the leading member of a gang who knew him as the 'Prince'. The business of this gang was, briefly, to acquire an interest in a firm, to stock it with inferior goods, to insure these goods at a grossly inflated rate, to set the firm's building on fire, and then to submit a fraudulent claim to the insurance company. Harris was said to have earned considerable sums of money from this unlawful enterprise, all or most of which he had lost in gambles on the stock exchange. At the time of the trial, he was faced, as Hatry had been, with bankruptcy.

Like Hatry, too, he pleaded guilty—or eventually he did—to all the charges against him, except for five cases of arson which he denied having had anything to do with. All but two of the gang were in the dock, and the chief witness for the prosecution was an Italian named Capsoni, a man of considerable charm of manner, who had himself been an important member. He was now being kept by the prosecution, for he was, he said, penniless, and it was explained that without his evidence there could have been no case brought against any of the defendants. The judge in his summing-up had some very hard things to say about Capsoni, and expressed regret that the man could not be punished as he 'richly deserved'. This lends some possibility of credence to a statement made by Harris years later that he fell in with some unscrupulous people and that he had 'paid his penalty'.

Nevertheless, Harris was convicted as the prime culprit, and he received by far the longest sentence. According to Harold Dearden in *The Fireraisers* (1934) his first known operation was in 1922, when he was 25 years old. The *Fabriques de Soieries* in Deansgate, Manchester, was deliberately set ablaze by Capsoni with the assistance of his wife-to-be. Harris was already in Manchester when the fire took place, and in due course collected £8,000 for himself.

This was followed by other similar ventures in various parts of the country, including a conflagration at 185 Oxford Street, London, as a result of which the Franco-Italian Silk Company was given its chance to file a claim, and which took place after the business had been transferred from premises in the Regent Arcade that were unfortunately found to be fire-proofed! Harris, who in legitimate cases was known for his enterprise in reaching the scene of a fire in front of his competitors, was invariably on the spot, or very close to it, before a fire was lit at his own instigation.

But, not surprisingly as the years went by, Harris's legitimate business suffered, because he himself had come under deeper and deeper suspicion; some of his fraudulent claims were either heavily slashed or, as in one instance, rejected outright. Yet despite these difficulties he was able to rely on two very powerful allies: Loughborough Ball, an insurance company representative, and Captain Miles of the Salvage Corps, both of whom offered their assistance. Ball received, for instance, £600 from the Franco-Italian Silk Company fire. Miles was not prosecuted with the rest of the gang. His trial came later after Harris himself had supplied information against him.

Harris's own fate was sealed when Capsoni decided to approach Mr William Crocker, an insurance solicitor, who had for several years past, as Harris knew, been assiduously collecting a dossier on the activities of the gang. The meetings between Capsoni and Crocker took place under conditions of elaborate secrecy, and eventually the latter was provided with sufficient information to present an iron-clad case.

Now it seemed certain to me that when Harris was sent to prison for fourteen years, that was the end of him—at least as a fire assessor. After all, here was a man who had not only submitted fraudulent claims but had committed arson in the process. What insurance company would ever be prepared to do business with him again? Besides, his credit was already close to nil before he and his gang were publicly exposed. According to Harold Dearden it would have been impractical for him to try to modify his malodorous reputation, which he had acquired before his conviction, by behaving honourably in the future, because 'you can't teach an old dog new tricks, especially when they happen to be violently opposed to every one of his instincts'. And if that was true then, or even if it wasn't, what earthly hope was there that anyone, either insurance company or client, could be persuaded to trust him again, even though he should come out of prison in his mid-forties still sound in body and mind?

I was given the answer to that question, quite by chance,

THE DAILY MIRROR, Tuesday, December 19, 1933

Broadcasting - Page 18

Daily Mirror

THE DAILY PICTURE NEWSPAPER WITH THE LARGEST NET SALE

BLOW TO THOUSANDS OF MOTORISTS —PAGE 3

No. 9,382 Registered at the G.P.O. as a Newspaper. TUESDAY, DECEMBER 19, 1933 One Penny

HARRIS ON '50 YEARS OF BRIBERY'

"Most of Salvage Corps Were in My Pay"

OFFICE CALLS FOR MONEY

SWEEPING new allegations were made by Leopold Harris, the fire raiser, at Bow-street yesterday in the charges against Captain Brynmor Eric Miles, chief of the London Salvage Corps.

Harris alleged that with very few exceptions the whole of the Salvage Corps were bribed by him.

Members would come openly to his office, sometimes in uniform, to receive

Leopold Harris, the fire raiser, who made further startling allegations during his cross-examination at Bow-street yesterday.

Daily Mirror, 19 December 1933

some thirty years later. Early one morning my two young children were playing with matches, and succeeded in setting an armchair alight. Fortunately the fire brigade arrived before the house went up in smoke, but some fairly serious damage was done to one room. 'You ought to get hold of Mr Leopold Harris', said the young fireman.

I thought he was joking. 'Why?' I asked casually. But then I realized how long ago that all was, and that this youth couldn't have been born when it happened. 'You mean you've heard of Leopold Harris?'

He hadn't. Not in the sense that I meant, and I didn't enlighten him. But he had heard of him as a fire assessor. He assured me he was the best in the business. Insurance companies had faith in him, and he could get me an excellent deal.

Afterwards, I made some enquiries of my own. I learned that upon his release from penal servitude over twenty years ago Leopold Harris had started up again as a fire assessor. He was at present doing very well. He had succeeded not only in modifying but in remodelling his reputation. He was accepted by every insurance company.

So I took the young fireman's advice, and employed Leopold Harris's firm to do my assessment. The result was perfectly satisfactory. More important, it was proof to me that some people, however few, can not only survive the tortures of prison unscathed, but can emerge from them the better for the experience.

BIBLIOGRAPHY

BARDENS, Dennis, *The Fall of Horatio Bottomley,* London 1972.
BELL, Daniel, *The End of Ideology,* New York 1960.
BUGLIOSI, Vincent, with GENTRY, Curt, *Helter Skelter,* New York 1974, London 1975.
BYRNE, Gerald, *Borstal Boy: The Uncensored Story of Neville Heath,* London 1947.
CRITCHLEY, MacDonald, ed., *The Trial of George Neville Clevely Heath,* London 1951.
DEARDEN, Harold, *The Fireraisers,* London 1934.
DEESON, Arthur F. L., *Great Swindlers,* London 1971.
EHRMANN, Herbert B., *The Case That Will Not Die,* New York 1970.
FAIRFIELD, Letitia, ed., *The Trial of Peter Barnes and Others,* London 1953.
FELIX, David, *Protest Sacco–Vanzetti and the Intellectuals,* New York 1965.
FORDHAM, Peta, *The Robbers' Tale,* London 1965.
FRANKAEL, Osmond K., *Sacco and Vanzetti,* New York 1931.
FRANKFURTER, Felix, *Sacco and Vanzetti,* New York 1927.
FRANKFURTER, Marion D., and JACKSON, Gardner, eds., *Letters of Sacco and Vanzetti,* New York 1928, London 1929.
HYMAN, Alan, *The Fall of Horatio Bottomley,* London 1972.
JACKSON, Robert, *The Chief: Life of Gordon Hewart,* London 1959.
JACKSON, Stanley, *Mr Justice Avory,* London 1935.
JENKINS, Peter M., *Mayfair Boy,* London 1952.
JENNINGS, Dean, *We Only Kill Each Other,* New York 1967, London 1969.
JOHNSON, James F. (as told to Floyd Miller), *The Man Who Sold the Eiffel Tower,* New York and London, 1962.
KOBLER, John, *Capone,* New York 1971, London 1972.
LYONS, Eugene, *The Life and Death of Sacco and Vanzetti,* New York 1928.
MORRIS, Norval, and HAWKINS, Gordon, *The Honest Politician's Guide to Crime Control,* Chicago and London, 1969.
MOULTON, H. Fletcher, ed., *The Trial of William Podmore,* London 1931.
O'KEEFE, J. J. (as told to Bob Considine), *The Crime That Nearly Paid,* New York 1962.
PAYNE, Leslie, *The Brotherhood,* London 1973.
PEARSON, John, *The Profession of Violence,* London 1972.
PLAYFAIR, Giles, and SINGTON, Derrick, *The Offenders,* New York and London, 1957.
—— *Crime, Punishment and Cure,* London 1965.
QUIN, Max C., *Dr Crippen,* London 1931.
ROOT, J., *The Betrayers,* New York 1964.
SHARP, Malcolm P., *Was Justice Done?,* New York 1956.
SONDERN, Frederick, *Brotherhood of Evil,* London 1959, New York 1960.
TALESE, Gay, *Honor Thy Father,* New York 1971, London 1972.
TURKUS, Burton B., with FEDER, Sid, *Murder Inc.,* New York 1950, London 1952.
WERTHAM, Fredric, *The Show of Violence,* New York 1948.
WEXLEY, John, *The Judgement of Julius and Ethel Rosenberg,* New York 1955.
WILLIAMS, Frank, *No Fixed Address,* London 1973.
YOUNG, Filson, ed., *The Trial of Hawley Harvey Crippen,* Edinburgh and London, 1920.

SOURCE NOTES

1 *The Times,* 17 September 1975.
2 London 1922.
3 *Brotherhood of Evil,* London 1959, New York 1960.
4 Burton B. Turkus with Sid Feder, New York 1950, London 1952.
5 *The End of Ideology,* New York 1960.
6 Chicago and London, 1969.
7 New York 1969.
8 New York 1968; published in London in 1969 under the title *The Canary That Sang.*
9 New York 1971, London 1972.
10 *Chicago Tribune,* 28 December 1974.
11 London and Boston, 1975.
12 *We Only Kill Each Other,* New York 1967, London 1969.
13 Quoted by Burton B. Turkus, op. cit.
14 New York 1963, London 1965.
15 Quoted by Dean Jennings, *We Only Kill Each Other,* New York 1967, London 1969.
16 Evidence before the Kefauver Committee on Crime given in New York, March 1951.
17 *The Profession of Violence,* London 1972.
18 *The Brotherhood,* London 1973.
19 *New York Times,* 11 August 1927.
20 Eugene Lyons, *The Life and Death of Sacco and Vanzetti,* New York 1928.
21 Quoted by Eugene Lyons, op. cit.
22 *Transcription of the record of the trial of Nicola Sacco and Bartolomeo Vanzetti in the courts of Massachusetts and subsequent proceedings, 1920–1927,* six vols., New York 1928.
23 Evidence of Professor James P. Richardson before Governor Fuller's Advisory Committee, 12 July 1927.
24 Transcription of trial.
25 Transcription of trial.
26 Quoted by Eugene Lyons, op. cit.
27 Transcription of trial.
28 Transcription of trial.
29 Article entitled 'Sacco and Vanzetti' which appeared in *Atlantic Monthly,* June 1927, and which was subsequently published in book form under the same title in New York in 1927.
30 *New York Times,* 11 August 1927.
31 Mark de Wolfe Howe, ed., *Holmes–Laski Letters,* London and New York, 1953.
32 *The World,* 12 May 1927.
33 Marion D. Frankfurter and Gardner Jackson, eds., *Letters of Sacco and Vanzetti,* New York 1928, London 1929.
34 From an article by W. E. Playfair, who was sole representative of the press at the execution (in 1927), published in the *Boston Herald,* August 1952.
35 ibid.
36 John Wexley, *The Judgement of Julius and Ethel Rosenberg,* New York 1955.
37 *Sunday Times,* 9 November 1975.
38 Letitia Fairfield, ed., *The Trial of Peter Barnes and Others,* London 1953.
39 ibid.

40 *The Trial of Hawley Harvey Crippen,* edited with notes and an introduction by Filson Young, Edinburgh and London, 1920.
41 ibid.
42 ibid.
43 Max C. Quin, *Dr Crippen,* London 1931.
44 New York 1948.
45 Fredric Wertham, *The Show of Violence,* New York 1948.
46 *Observer,* 8 May 1966.
47 Dennis Bardens, *The Ladykiller,* London 1972.
48 Quoted by Gerald Byrne, *Borstal Boy : The Uncensored Story of Neville Heath,* London 1947.
49 MacDonald Critchley, ed., *The Trial of George Neville Clevely Heath,* London 1961.
50 New York 1974, London 1975.
51 Vincent Bugliosi with Curt Gentry, *Helter Skelter,* New York 1974, London 1975.
52 Bugliosi with Gentry, op. cit.
53 ibid.
54 ibid.
55 ibid.
56 ibid.
57 *Mayfair Boy,* London 1952.
58 Quoted by Robert Jackson, *The Chief : Life of Gordon Hewart,* London 1959.
59 Quoted by Peta Fordham, *The Robbers' Tale,* London 1965.
60 London 1973.
61 Quoted by Peta Fordham, op. cit.
62 New York and London, 1962.
63 Quoted by Alan Hyman, *The Fall of Horatio Bottomley,* London 1972.
64 ibid.
65 *The Times,* 2 August 1922.
66 Quoted by Stanley Jackson, *Mr Justice Avory,* London 1935.
67 25 January 1930.

INDEX

References to pages on which illustrations appear are in italics
'n' refers to footnotes

Acknowledgements
All pictures are reproduced by permission of Popperfoto with the exception of those on the following pages: pp. 95, 128 (insets), 150 (inset), 156, British Library Board, photo: Chris Barker; 128, Central Press; 20 (inset), 58 (inset), 66, 70, 78, 79, 89 (right), 110 (top), 124, 134, 140, 142–3 (top), 149, 160 (top), 164 (bottom left), 169, John Frost; 94, Radio Times Hulton Picture Library.